MYTHS THAT RULE AMERICA

**Herbert I. London
Albert L. Weeks**

University Press
of America™

Myths That Rule America

Table of Contents

page

Preface vii
Prologue ix
About Us 3
Chapter
1. Myth of Absolute Freedom 5
2. Myth of Happiness 11
3. Myth of Success 3
4. Myth of Equality 24
5. Myth of Technology 31
6. Myth of Small Is Beautiful 37
7. Myth of Work 43
8. Myth of Poverty 50
9. Myth of Psychology 56
10. Myth of Experimental Art 61
11. Myth of Impotence 66
About Others 73
12. Myth of World Community 75
13. Myth of "MIC" 82
14. Myth of Ideology 92
15. Myth of Peace 101
16. Myth of Isolationism 112
About "Others" 121
17. Myth of Geopolitics 124
18. Myth of "ETI" 135
Conclusion 145
19. Faith and Will 147
Glossary 155

PREFACE

In our judgment, myths can be useful or they can be destructive. They can engender efforts of Olympian quality, or they may inspire inertia and vindictiveness. In the last two decades, the myths that have mushroomed in the dark and fetid confusion of the late 1960's have created a basis for present impotence and cynicism.

This book is not mere description of the current climate of opinion, or *Zeitgeist*. Instead, it is an antidote to fatuous social policy and prevalent orthodoxies, all of which act as harmful myth. It is our considered opinion that what this nation requires is a positive and useful myth of faith and collective will, a restatement of our national purpose as it affects affairs both at home and abroad.

Many books about myth are on library shelves. Ours, however, is the first to recognize the *functional use of myth* as a clarification of reality and as a spur to creative activity. If the utility and perniciousness of certain contemporary myths are perceived by the reader, the goal of the authors will have been achieved.

Our book is likely to upset some readers. So be it. We make no bones about our desire to be provocative. Frankly, we have written a polemic. So, let the chips, and the flak, fall where they may.

H I L
A L W

*Note: Chapters 1-11 were written by Herbert I. London; Chapters 12-18, by Albert L. Weeks. The Prologue, Conclusion, and Glossary are joint ventures.

Prologue

> ". . . worlds are made not only by what is said literally but also by what is said metaphorically . . ."
>
> Nelson Goodman

This book is a polemic, from the Greek, *polemos,* meaning war. The word fits because, frankly, we are engaged in combat with a number of contemporary enemies. True, the adversaries may be as invisible as Don Quixote's windmills. But they are no less dangerous for their being will-o-the-wisp.

The enemy is myth, but more precisely, those myths that are pernicious. It is our contention that a number of harmful myths are being deployed today to explain and make sense of both national and international affairs. Unfortunately, numerous attitudes and policies were, and continue to be, developed on the basis of myth in the areas of public opinion and decision making in Congress and in the White House. In many instances the policies are unsuccessful because they are ill-conceived in the first place. They are ill-conceived because they rely so heavily on erroneous assumptions.

It may sound strange for the authors to emphasize that not all myths are harmful. The fact is that a country needs useful myths the way an individual needs unprovable assumptions on which to base his or her personal behavior. The bible, for example, speaks of basing Christian behavior on the assumptions of faith, hope and charity. All such assumptions must be, in a sense, mythical; they are certainly "intangible" in the crudely materialistic sense — a materialism, by the way, which is itself part of contemporary epistemological myth-making. After all, you cannot weigh faith, or hope, or love, although St. Augustine maintained that his "weight" was his love of God. Just as religion rests on intangible assumptions, nations rely on hypostatized principles to determine policy. The principles, the ideas, the myths, the value-impregnated assumptions — all rather fantastically "create" reality. As they direct that reality into its deepest channels, they act like so many hidden hands manipulating a stage-full of puppets.

Our book exposes and combats the misguiding myths and the misguided myth-makers, and the consequences stemming from the pernicious myths that have been generated in contemporary society. This involves a somewhat difficult "demythologizing," or therapeutic, process that is essential to an understanding of public policy.

Most myths have become habits of mind that intrude on our actions yet are rarely discernible. Habits of mind, however, are fundamental, even when some of the manifestations are perverse. For example, the basic function of astrology is to substitute a religion of substance for a religion of fatuous symbols. The Ram, The Twins, or Jupiter's "box" are infused with the dignity of church dogma, but ultimately they are silly and simplistic. The "science" of astrology is even sillier: that the sun, moon, stars, and planets send out rays influencing our behavior in this or that way, on a daily, even hourly basis. Many people confuse the meaning of words — in this case, "astrology" — with its legitimate sound-alike, "astronomy." It is precisely this kind of verbal confusion that often underwrites myth in its negative connotation. An official in the government of the City of New York, according to a *New York Times* interview, seriously maintained that the hiring of people to work in urban government should be based in part upon astrological information — e.g., their "sun-signs" — contained in their vitaes. If people can be so foolish as to believe in astrology — beliefs that surely can produce a potent effect on them and their relation to others, not to mention children brought up to believe in the postulates of their particular "sun-signs" — what else might they believe in?

Myths can be decidedly useful. But often, they become perverted by "realist" attempts to interpret their mythic message literally. Take the mythic statement of the American Declaration of Independence. It states that we are born equal, with certain "inalienable" rights, among which are life, liberty and the pursuit of happiness. The statement contains the ruling democratic myth about equality. But even a child knows that he is not equal to his brother — most likely, in strength. He will soon find out too, that people are notoriously unequal in talents, as well as talons. But if he continues to accept the naive proposition that equality is "inherent" or "tangible," disillusionment inevitably sets in along with the claim that he became unequal to others only because of "unequal opportunity." (But since when are opportunities found ready-made, except at gambling casinos, and even then in very small amounts? Opportunities, as Branch Rickey often said, are *made,* not ready-made.) Laboring under the misapprehension that disadvantage is fostered solely by "environment" can itself be a disabling, harmful myth. For the surest way of actually becoming unsuccessful in one's work and career is to invent myths which appear to "explain," but only succeed in retarding, individual advancement.

This is no less true of whole nations. If we assumed that all men and women were *not* created equal, that *no* providential power gave them their inalienable rights, those very men and women would soon find themselves living in a nation without rights. Likewise, some social theoreticians have based their assumptions about society and politics on the argument (also a myth) that the State, or the Revolution, has given men and women their rights; in their view, there is no "God," no source for rights other than the Party, the State, the Revolution, the Leader. To the unthoughtful many, these sources of rights sound, unfortunately, far more "tangible" than the "fiction" about God or "God-given right."

Note the devastating effect of a denial of God-given rights. Under right-wing or left-wing totalitarianism, there is no place for a "higher source" of rights other than real-life leaders and ideologies. God has been banished on the grounds that He is a useless even harmful myth, or as Lenin said, "spiritual vodka for the masses." What Lenin, and the whole train of materialistic, and those empiricist thinkers who have so deformed present-day mentalities worldwide have maintained, is that whatever we know, on whatever grounds we base national principles and behavior, should be "concrete" and subject to "science." In almost every one of their speeches, Leonid Brezhnev or Fidel Castro describes the Communist ideology as a "science." This sets up a confusion far more harmful in scope than the one about astrology. In Marxist-Leninist "science," God becomes a childish fantasy; the "realities" are provided by the ideology, the

Revolution, the Party — ultimately of course, the coercive power of the State.

While myth, as so far described, is sometimes a negative construct, it is nevertheless an idea that occurs in a particular space and time and which provides a symbolic representation for social action. It may be observed as a naive view of reality, as poetic imagination or as truth. But whatever the nature of the perception, myth invariably contains a cherished memory that captivates the imagination.

In all times, myths have flourished and served as the inspiration for the more sweeping manifest ideas that have sprung from the human mind. Joseph Campbell's view of myth is unquestionably hyperbolic but nonetheless revealing: "Myth is the secret opening through which the inexhaustible energies of the cosmos pour into human cultural manifestation."

Myth has many explanations, but the transmogrification of a character or an idea into a myth involves a process of faith that most often defies empirical proof or evidence. Icarus flies, Galahad vanquishes his foes, and Helen mystifies because we want or need these conditions as a projection of reality. Those projections that transcend reality serve as myth precisely when they inspire conduct that either shatters or supports the prevailing order of things.

Malinowski contended that every element of a culture should be presumed to have a function until proven otherwise. There are instances where ideas appear to be legitimate; they have the backing of a scientific consensus and new findings may even confer permanency upon them. And yet, they remain partly mythological. For example, the Newtonian model of the physical world was irreparably modified by Einsteinian theory. Can anyone "visualize" Einstein's continuum, or curved space, or infinite instant-point, or "Nows"? Is it not mind-boggling, in any literal sense, to conceive of the deceleration and contraction of time for passengers on a space ship traveling near the speed of light? If there is no simultaneity and no before-this or after-this in relations between widely-separated events in outer space, do not our earth-bound simultaneities and timing become illusory?

The fact is, of course, that no two places, even within the same "Time Zone," have the same time. Time is determined by the "passage" of the sun overhead, but these solar beams constantly move — about 1,000 mph, as a matter of fact. How, then, can Syracuse and New York City, although said to be in the same Time Zone, actually enjoy the same time: We merely mythologize their relationships and overlook the fact that New

York City actually has somewhat later time (because it's east of Syracuse) than does Syracuse. Cities separated by hundreds of miles within the same time zone could vary as much as a half hour in time if we made different assumptions about their relationship. In other words, the sensate, measurable "reality" is one thing; what we choose to make of it, how we choose to think of it, another.

It is also true that myth can have utility in the maintenance of social equilibrium. The frontier myth in nineteenth century history created an illusion of unbounded opportunity which partially defused antagonistic political elements and reinforced the status quo. On the other hand, the replacement of the Horatio Alger myth with a myth of success based on political influence or chance, has led to a disincentive for hard work and for honorable behavior. It is also a potentially disintegrating force in a culture where rewards for labor are evaluated with skepticism, a skepticism that undermines the labor itself.

It should be recalled that myth and reality intersect at the point when men act as if the myth were true and base their beliefs and actual conduct upon it. What is one person's myth is another's reality. All people — to some degree — live in accordance with norms and principles that have been drawn from myth. It is therefore the recognition and understanding of myth that is essential for political analysis.

Interestingly, some cultures intentionally mythologize for particular political ends. In "The Search for A Usable Past" Henry Steele Commager claims that Americans in the nineteenth century set out "with a vengeance to create a usable past," which included most obviously the creation of myths. Myths are so essential to our culture that if they did not exist, like Voltaire's God, they would have to be invented. They represent certainties in an otherwise uncertain world. And when they are shattered by disuse or doubt, the effect may be cataclysmic.

In our own age, we have become so enamoured of allegedly "rational" ideas buttressed by scientific logic and empirical "evidence" that we intentionally debunk myths, or we replace the ones that were seemingly irrational with "new" rational ones. In the nineteenth century, along with a faith in Darwinian assumptions, there emerged the myth of progress. It was expressed in a variety of ways typified by the belief in "manifest destiny," but with unerring certainty, it replaced the old, "irrational" faith in a providential plan of the future.

Similarly, for much of the last century, and in this

one, progress was synonomous with optimism, excluding temporary aberrations, such as the period of disenchantment immediately after World War I. If the conditions were not as we wished them, one could expect improvement to come in the future. This was an affirmative, activist orientation that imparted tone and purpose and a driving energy to the society. Since 1950 with the introduction of nuclear armaments, the Cold War and, most importantly, a perception of apocalypse occurring at any moment, the dominant myth of optimism has surrendered in most quarters to a belief in pessimism and defeat, and to the myths that give rise to them. In fact, Schopenhauer's world-view of "ominous quiescence" now characterizes much of American mythology. We are unhinging the bonds that affirm life and are substituting entropy and negation.

While this may seem an extreme interpretation, we hedge by suggesting that this condition is only a contemporary trend supported by a system of beliefs that contains all the frightening elements of Prometheus *unbound*. By so emphasizing sensate pragmatism, the culture, with varying degrees of emphasis, contends that there are no truths, except those derived from the facts of social life, economics, sensation and desire. The human spirit is seemingly tied to material things and is held inexorably in the grip of facts. There is no room or imagination for transcendence and, consequently, no inspiration or heroism. The notion that this state of affairs is "normal" possesses its own idiosyncratic rationality and has itself become another of the contemporary myths.

When functioning properly, myth provides social control and encourages activity. It moves political systems to heights of achievement and beneficence. But when it is dysfunctional, it can produce a fury of inhuman destruction. It is at once essential to ethics, while also giving rise to immorality on a scale that in our century has left permanent scars in civilization's memory.

In other words, myth may become part of our dream of glory, or it may become our nightmare. It may allow our political system to cohere, or it may prove an ever-present enemy to our institutions. On one issue, however, there is probably consensus: Wherever there is human civilization, no matter how invisible or intangible, myth inevitably accompanies it. This happens because people require myths not only as an "escape from reality," but to give meaning and direction to reality. As R. M. McIver has said, "Myth is the all-pervading atmosphere of society, the air it breathes."

As we have suggested, myth affects the entire tenor of our lives. If Horatio Alger was a workable myth at some point, it was because this nineteenth-century fiction embodied values that people wished whole-heartedly to embrace. The fiction buttressed the values that in turn influenced the evolution of the social and economic system.

Horatio Alger's young characters evidenced honesty, dedication, and hard work and were rewarded with success. While these young men were a model of capitalist enterprise, they were the symbol of mythic community virtue. Above all, Horatio Alger's characters were honorable people. Even when personal advantage could be gained from dissimulation or silence, they would forego self-aggrandizement for the preservation of virtuous behavior.

The Horatio Alger myth served two useful functions: It promoted the idea that hard work will lead to success and it established the moral parameters for business activity. In a real sense this view was the secular manifestation of the Protestant Ethic. Good works make the good man and goodness is a transcendent value related to moral precepts.

Similarity, individualism, which De Tocqueville described in the early part of the nineteenth century, as "egoistic" behavior, came to be identified with personal initiative at a time when industrialization was being introduced on a large scale. The evolution of this myth suggests several incarnations: from egoism to Emersonian self-reliance to Hooverian "rugged individualism." This change in perception reflected a change in social demands. Independence became a positive value when it was a requisite for economic enterprise. When cooperative urges had to be encouraged — as was the case in the establishment of western settlements — individualism was considered personal aggrandizement obtained at the expense of social cohesion. In this matter — as well as many other cases — reality and myth blend into a new awareness of social phenomena.

"Individualism" — "independence" — "initiative" — these are words locked into a mythic history of the nation. Their special ritualistic functions ignore rational argument. Frankly, they are eulogistic terms, mere words pegged into the timetable of history. They represent our moods and needs. And at times they function as incentives for national policies.

The mythic structure is dynamic — some would argue it is less dynamic and more subject to fad. In our own time individualism has been employed as a way to oppose government intrusion in our lives, e.g. Ayn Rand's *The Virtue of Selfishness* and as an expression of youthful nonconformity, e.g., the ethos of "do your own thing." Seemingly, the myth has been transformed to suit our social occasions.

In perhaps a similar sense, the word "frontier" has been mythologized by historical and fictional interpretations. Frederick Jackson Turner romanticized the frontier idea in his classic histories of the West. Today's media producers have carried Turner's work to its mythic extreme. The West has become the symbol of American boldness as much because of Roy Rogers and Hopalong Cassidy as any actual settlers. Our vision has been blurred by the magnification of the camera. What we see, of course, are heroes who can solve issues with a fast draw; opportunities available for anyone with guts and complex issues reduced to the Manichaean world of good and bad guys.

Yet, the tangible frontier of the West, which was declared closed in the census of 1890, has been transformed into "new," invisible, fictionalized, (mythologized) frontiers of the twentieth century. The frontiers have become intangible. The myth of the Western frontier has been replaced by the frontier of technology. An axial expansion of knowledge has forced us to the brink of technical advances so sophisticated that their implications have become our collective nightmare. The frontier myth, with all its attendant opportunities, has surrendered to the technical myth of Frankenstein's monster.

Curiously, a myth, while beneficial in its application, may often evoke extreme interpretations that change it into a pernicious myth. Thomas Jefferson's "pursuit of happiness" phrase is an appropriate illustration. This expression in the Declaration of Independence implies liberty to pursue satisfaction within a community of shared values. Presumably, the "happiness" is dependent not only on seeking personal goals, but on acknowledging one's relationship to the accepted standards of the community. In this sense, the pursuit of happiness is both personal and social. But this myth — on which communal well-being depended — has been perverted in today's atmosphere of narcissism into happiness at any price, even if it means severing one's ties to the social system. Happiness and its pursuit — in its contemporary construction — are considered a solely personal venture. "If the world cannot accomodate my desire, then it should change, not I." In its logical extrapolation, this position is but another form of updated utilitarianism. But instead of "the greatest good for the greatest number," the hedonist now argues for "the greatest good for me." The result is a pernicious belief that in the aggregate, narrow self-concern will cohere into social consciousness. Unfortunately, a sizable segment of the population rationalizes narcissistic action as compatible with the mythic pursuit of happiness.

As myth affects our attitudes, the reality of the contemporary scene affects our myth. We are caught in the dilemma of requiring myth to make our reality meaningful. Without God's law man cannot be released from the limitations of personal vanity. This position is based on the human need to control extreme behavior through the influence of a transcendent morality. Natural law is an invocation to fear, to behold and to act. Without transcendence there is little likelihood of enduring social unity. For human flaws invariably translate into their social parallel: Personal avarice has as its social counterpart the totalitarian state, and a lack of personal discipline reveals itself as anarchy. If every person — through his shared humanity — is presumed to be qualified to rule, the social system will reflect only the will of those who can control. God is indeed necessary, not only as a religious exemplar, but as a practical premise for the politics of liberty.

All mythologies contain a vision of what we aspire to be and have within them the purgatory of destructive thoughts. Myth illumines and projects a light in the darkness of reality and the haze of misperception over the glow of truth. It is our task to distinguish between those myths that give us light and those that blind our vision.

MYTHS
THAT
RULE
AMERICA

ABOUT US . . .

Chapter 1

The Myth of Absolute Freedom

> "Society cannot exist unless a controlling power upon will
> and appetite be placed somewhere, and the less of it there is
> within, the more there must be without."
>
> **Edmund Burke**

Entering my consciousness like a half-forgotten dream is a song that was part of my pre-adolescent memory bank: "The Best Things in Life Are Free." There was nothing particularly haunting about the melody and the lyrics were nonsensical, but it did establish my faith in a mystical kind of freedom. For if the best things are free, then freedom must be free. The logic is somewhat convoluted but what can you expect from a ten-year-old who imbibed pop music lyrics the way most kids devoured ice cream sandwiches? When I would say things that would prompt my contemporaries to shout "hey you can't say that," I would steadfastly reply, "I can say whatever I please; this is a free country." So well had I learned my lyrical lesson that I was an unwitting defender of absolute freedoms long before I even heard of Justice Black. It was also a time before I considered the ramifications of my posturing. I simply looked at an American flag and thought of *my* freedom.

It wasn't until I reached high school that the matter of freedom became somewhat engimatic. One day as I walked through the corridors of Jamaica High School two thugs stopped me and requested my change in language that I used exclusively in school yard basketball games. Since I had walked two miles to school in order to save the fifteen cent carfare, I wasn't about to give up my change to an army of King Kongs much less these two thugs. So when I said, "no way," they started to pummel my stomach and face until one teacher who had the courage to intervene said, "Enough!" When this teacher asked for an explanation, these thugs said "None of ya business; this is a free country." It was exactly at that moment that freedom began to mean something different from the notion in my naive past. It is also this scene at Jamaica High School that I recall everytime I hear the Oliver Wendell Holmes Jr. quotation, "Your freedom ends where my nose begins." My nose could testify to the judgment.

From this episode it is rather easy to understand why I was so sensitive to the intrinsic excesses of freedom. It wasn't that I loved freedom any the less, only that I recognized with a certain poignancy what it can become without limitation. It was this lesson that I returned to many a time thereafter.

Like most college youths educated at a liberal university in the fifties, I was entranced by the apparent verities of existentialism. "Life is meaningless" I told unwary girls on park benches only half understanding the full import of my claims. And I'm not even sure which half I understood — the existence or the essence. I read and repeated lines from Albert Camus with all the gravity I could muster. It was during one of my several readings of *The Rebel* that I rediscovered what I intuitively considered true. "There is no justice;" noted Camus, "there is only limitation." Could it be, I asked myself, that Camus meant to say freedom instead of justice? It would have been consistent with this text, moreover it seemed to me the real controversy undergirding rebellion. Freedom exists only with its inherent contradiction. A rebel without a cause is like Jimmy Dean and the thugs at Jamaica High School: a threat to others and ultimately a threat to the freedom that gave them license.

This analysis of the precarious character of freedom is by no means new. It is simply a case of balancing those shibboleths learned in school with the truths of the street. "Of course freedom has limits," shout dissenters who won't let me respond. It was always freedom for them and limits for me. Events in the sixties and seventies confirm this observation. The children of Woodstock learned — perhaps overlearned — the value of freedom, but they didn't learn about restraint. When, as a professor, I engaged students in discussion, I was at a distinct disadvantage. They were free to say what they wished; I, on the other hand, was encumbered by proprieties and a well-developed sense of fair play. When they would shout "bull shit," I would say, "What is the evidence for your claims?" It is obvious who got the better of those exchanges.

As Freud has noted, freedom must be restrained through the development of a conscience. Yet those weaned on the Con III value of "let it all hang out" considered conscience a trick of the Establishment to ensure social order. And they are right. Conscience does mean order, but it is as much a trick of the Establishment — whatever that is — as the belief that concentration in order to learn something is a trick of the F.B.I. to keep you out of trouble. If desire is not harnessed, the pleasure principle is subject solely to utilitarian standards. Consider this extrapolation. If in the act of rape the rapist derives 20 units of pleasure, compared to ten units of displeasure he gives the person being raped, his freedom to act seems socially desirable. This syllogism is logical, but the initial assumption is wrong. There are simply some acts that shouldn't be done regardless of the pleasure obtained. Rapists, of course, don't know that; neither do these *enfant terribles* of the sixties who performed their deeds with extraordinary vanity and little regard for restraint.

"Do your thing" often meant reject the uptight standards of the public (read: bourgeois) conscience. In the afterglow of university riots, expression was everything. Freedom became an absolute right in the puerile minds that were sure laws only secure the advantage of the privileged class. Since most of these rebels were members of that class, there was something paradoxical about the claim. Yet this view was more than an adolescent beating on his chest for an emergent manhood. Freedom without restraint was fast becoming a goal of the larger society in the same way my adolescent belief in doing what I wanted made what I wanted worth doing. This analogy is not so far fetched. With adolescence extended into the thirties, it is not unusual to find aging students who maintain that their desires *must* be recognized. One student, confusing himself with Patrick Henry, told my class that "even if what I want is wrong, my importance as a human being warrants consideration of my desires." Indeed! Then all human beings who by virtue of their birth are important, have desires that warrant consideration. This was not what the Founding Fathers had in mind when they spoke of unalienable rights.

If freedom is equated with desire — as is often the case — then in the tradition of musical comedy, anything goes. Laws are subordinated to feelings of satisfaction. The hero of *Clockwork Orange* is a prototype for the "new freedom." His cruel acts make him feel good, so why not do them? Is it any wonder that our criminals, when they are apprehended, consider themselves "political prisoners." After all, the society guarantees their freedom — or so it is naively believed — why then should their actions be punished?

With free expression of every variety a possibility and with solipsism the only consideration holding rein "I can do what you can't" is the operating principle. At the height of the sixties turmoil when I was told that dropping out was the only answer — an answer to what I cannot say — I decided to find my Eden at a commune. I visited a place in Vermont where it was maintained freedom was the underlying, guiding principle of organization. This freedom applied to free love, as well as to free choice. In fact, the freedom was largely a matter of interpretation. The leader — a man who was not elected but selected as if by providential will — told me that I must "share my woman." I thought that he meant the mutual sharing of women. However, that was an egregious error. My sexual freedom ended where his bevy of women began. He was free by virtue of some subtle authority I wasn't privy to; while I had freedom when it was granted. This noticeably one-sided agreement didn't particularly bother anyone but me, until the leaders' group of women grew to such proportions that only he and several privileged males had sexual freedom. It was at precisely that moment that the communal experiment with free sex came to an end. As one adherent noted "freedom emanates from George's (our leader's) authority." I still use that example as a rather perverse definition of freedom.

As I recount these experiences, I recall Irving Kristol's argument that "whole classes of the population . . . are entering what can only be called, in the strictly clinical sense, a phase of infantile regression." "I won't take no for an answer" is heard as a rallying cry for a generation of libertarians. With Abraham Maslow, as its spiritual father, the movement demands self actualization which usually takes the form of self indulgence. How can I be a better person, it is argued, if I am not permitted self-expression? To hell with two hundred years of this American social contract. Who cares about four thousand years of civilization? "I must find myself;" "I must grow;" "I must be able to understand myself." As the assertions become more vigorous, so does the embrace of freedom as an absolute value. The encounter leader usually tells his congregants "feel free, open up, express yourself." Of course, when Humpty Dumpty has his great fall, he's not around to pick up the pieces. After all, he's only doing his thing.

Perhaps "autonomous man" has always been a social goal. Perhaps people always rebelled against inhibition and guilt. Perhaps civilization always struggled with the primitive pleasure giving experience of destruction. Yet, while I recognize my own prejudices, I still can't help but feel that restraints are being eroded in an unprecedented way. In the hope of liberating man from cultural repression, it is the inhibitions that we are losing. Psychiatrists — by no means all psychiatrists but a fair number I submit — tell their patients "to do what makes you feel good." What makes many people feel good may make me feel bad, but I'm not that psychiatrist's patient — not yet anyway. In the process, social cohesion becomes less cohesive; and morality is determined by people of the couch not those of the cloth.

Where does this lead? The search for absolute freedom is irresistible. Yet, ironically, it also creates frustrations. For if man is free, why associate with those who, by virtue of the association, limit that freedom? The natural concomitant of this argument is that those who are free are also without associations. Any relationship — be it with a mate or a friend or a group — presumes some degree of commitment and concern for others. But "autonomous man" must guard his freedom against control. As a consequence the price for freedom is loneliness. Divorce rates soar as each of the mates considers himself a free spirit. And institutions like Esalen are then created for the free spirits to come together. Curiously, when these free spirits do find meaning through associations they exhibit a loyalty that borders on zealotry. Those free spirits of the sixties who paraded aimlessly through Haight Ashbury became perfect subjects for totalitarian control in the seventies. In far too many cases to be happenstance, the flower children who sought freedom with a vengeance chose a life with the Reverend Moon, the Maharishi, or more grotesquely than the others, with Charles Manson. For them a ten-year odyssey led freedom to the sacrificial altar of "the purposeful life."

Clearly, freedom is, to some extent, relative. But as it is perceived as a rigid, absolute value it ceases to have vitality. My father, who learned about freedom on the streets of the East Side two generations ago, used to say that "if a man is free to do whatever he wants, I don't count my change outdoors." That's a translation from the Yiddish, but the point is obvious in any language. With freedom's meaning unraveled, with many people in society unwilling to accept conventional restraints, freedom as we've known it has lost her loveliness. We are in jeopardy of losing this value completely at the same time that we vocally defend its importance.

Chapter 2

The Myth of Happiness

"One is never as happy or as unhappy as one thinks."
La Rochefoucauld

"Happiness . . . is a perpetual possession of being well deceived . . . the serene and peaceful state of being a fool among knaves."

Jonathan Swift

"A lifetime of happiness! It should be hell on earth."
G. B. Shaw

If there is one chimera that all Americans pursue it is happiness. Every wishbone torn by dreamers of the future or coins wishfully dropped in a fountain invariably contain the mythic desire for happiness. The word represents our presumptive bliss, an ectasy that transcends the limits of our biology. Yet, happiness cannot be sustained. It fades once the cause of the happiness loses its vigor or novelty.

In our time, happiness is a function of tangible gain. It has been reified by the emphasis on materialism. Happiness is that new car, or a house in the suburbs or perhaps winning the lottery. We have taken an abstraction and made it concrete through our desire for more — ever more — things.

Instead of envisioning happiness as it really is — a shooting star that catches our eye momentarily — we wish to grasp it and hold on. Contentment, which is in my opinion the higher state of satisfaction, does not have the momentary glow of happiness, but does have the sustained pleasure of tranquility. Unfortunately, in a culture stimulated by the media, contentment is viewed as complacency, a state wholly unsuited to the changing times.

It was once argued that happiness for the older man included: faster horses, younger women, older whiskey and more money. Now the goal is widely embraced — with, of course, younger men the goal of the older female. Happiness has become the ubiquitous search for more at any price, a condition that accentuates our greed and diminishes our charity. The poor argue that the privilege of more money is their right; the middle class maintain that keeping what they have earned is their preference and the rich contend that investing what is theirs is an entitlement. If these assumptions are at all accurate, the goal of happiness has increased the struggle between groups and as a consequence has opened a Pandora's Box of irreconcilable personal fulfillments.

The idea of mythical happiness obtained through possessions or personal fulfillment has relatively recent origins. Moreover, it is a reflection of a culture divorced from the past, impatient with tradition, lacking in taste and bewildered by it's ephemeral values. Happiness doesn't mitigate the effect of change or serve as a symbol of order and continuity in which people can find repose. It is instead the bellweather of change itself; it's "what's happening." A standard of order has been replaced by the personal goal of happiness: "If I think it will make me happy, it therefore must be good." The "it" in this sentence can be anything from a weekend in Fire Island to a leather case at Gucci's. This self-indulgence that challenges traditional norms at every turn now masquerades as the valid pursuit of happiness. A responsive marketplace in its desire to accommodate this opinion makes ever more elaborate gestures to form and style, while substance is ignored. Although there are a myriad of factors that account for this phenomenon — including most obviously the erosion of normative social standards — there are specific reasons that in my view are culprits in this examination: revolutionary politics; a loss of cultural meaning; and an emphasis on anarchic freedom.

The revolutionary fervor of our times demands the spread of a world-immanent gospel in order to achieve personal happiness. Politicize culture, so the argument suggests, and you help politicize people. Those conditions that produce quiet joy and catharsis, instead of fostering the "sense of injured merit" (the phrase is credited to Henry James) and inciting the revolutionary appetite, are deemed antithetical to happiness. In this way traditional standards are vitiated by the "new standard" of the social-political aesthetic: Propaganda confuses compassion, tact, kindness, and discipline with escapism, decadence, and despair.

As the nation is increasingly concerned about what it is, it stands to reason that one manifestation of the dilemma is the loss of consensual values, what many have loosely called the loss of cultural meaning. In search of a belief system that is forever undermined, Americans look to their culture for answers. But that culture is a mirror-image of prevailing values; and the one value that remains constant is a belief in change. The result is the mutually-contradictory values of change as a reflection of principles in the marketplace and "standards" as those cluster of ideas that require stability, continuity and consensual values. Cultural standards that rest on stability for their contribution to the quality of life are at odds with the utilitarian principle of temporary goals for commercial enrichment.

The contemporary social analyst is inclined to assume that happiness is perforce a function of absolute freedom above all else. For the neo-libertarian, freedom is indeed imperative. But as Proust, among others, has argued, without the prerequisite of discipline and a shared understanding of social controls, unrestrained freedom is inevitably destructive. Ultimately, the freedom so treasured by the culture depreciates into an anarchy that values only the ephemeral.

A purely selfish view of the pursuit of happiness that makes one man's quest as valid as the next is leading to no standards at all. That is the course we are on. In this case, as in so many others, real progress must take the form of rediscovery. It may very well be that what the revolutionists suggest we reject is precisely what should be embraced.

As Eric Voegelin has suggested, any rebel who wishes to think rationally and find the contentment he allegedly is seeking, needs only "to turn around and toward that reality against which the symbols of rebellion aggress." The point is that the actual guideline for the seeker may be in the act of rebellion if the rebel realizes that what he is seeking may be found in that against which he rebels. In a somewhat different, yet relevant analogue, psychologists contend that those people with phobias may actually be seeking that which is seemingly repulsive. The claustrophobe may actually desire the warmth and intimacy of a close relationship. The acrophobe may simply want to fly free, reaching heights where he can't be restrained. It is illustrative, I believe, that many Soviet labor camp prisoners experience a life-affirming spiritual force precisely at the brink of personal annihilation. The experience in the Gulag forced a rethinking of behavioral psychology and Marxism, the sustaining symbols of modern philosophy. An intense, concentrated life in which death is imminent at any moment made life oddly precious and beyond the understanding of determinism or the behaviorist's cast iron influence of environment on behavior.

If one had to identify the time when alienation — to use a much abused word — came to be associated with modernism, it was not at the point when advanced technology was introduced, albeit that fact of history cannot be underestimated, or when affluence became an accepted condition of American life. Alienation as an expression of widespread unhappiness can best be interpreted — it seems to me — as an expression of the Nietzschean belief in the death of God and the absurdity of an afterlife.

In a religious tradition contentment is the combination of virtue and free will that takes into account the rewards and punishments of heaven and hell in an afterlife. Presumably, this religious tradition is rooted in the weight of future glory that makes immediate virtue enriching in its purpose and *inter alia* the best bargain one can obtain. Pascal contended that the mere probability of an afterlife should encourage reasonable people to follow God's will so that they might enjoy the eternal happiness of heaven rather than attempt to satisfy the uneasiness of our desires pursuing trifling matters on earth. However, once this tradition was eroded by the prophets of rationality who required concrete evidence of an afterlife, there was nothing left but secular pursuits. In renouncing the afterlife, we were left at the mercy of our own desires. Genuine satisfaction became forever beyond our grasp, always contingent and yet another cloud in our confused state.

With the so-called death of God and the consequent cynicism about an afterlife, virtuous behavior has become little more than a residual, anachronistic formulation whose antecedents are made unclear by present concerns. Moreover, the calculus of freedom and virtue as the sum of happiness is now reduced to freedom alone. What increases my freedom increases my happiness. This new interpretation of utilitarianism has made personal will and willfulness the only avenue to the goal of happiness. Yet, as has already been noted, freedom without restraint is ultimately no freedom and certainly no happiness at all.

Of course, there is also the perverse side to spiritual loyalty and an afterlife as a source of happiness. As the legitimate institutions have become delegitimized the search for orthodoxies that will give life meaning becomes overpowering. As cynicism intrudes on rational approaches to social solutions, mysticism of every conceivable variety fills the vacuum left by the abandonment of rationality. As people feel helpless to cope with the demands of the modern age they become ever more vulnerable to charismatic leaders. The mass suicide in Jonestown, Guyana, was but an extreme episode in the contemporary desire for apocalyptic redemption. For Jones' followers there was a belief that health, wealth and especially happiness could be discovered in his messianic faith. Jones made the human wreckage in his community believe that the dead can be reborn, that one's enemies will be defeated, that heaven on earth can be created, and that dying for the People's Temple is a way to assure oneself eternal happiness.

Clearly, faith without reason can lead to human automatons, divorced from truth and reality. And reason without faith can bewilder the soul, creating a wasteland of things that add little to life's genuine happiness. In a recent article about this question Richard Easterlin concluded that as "each person acts on the assumption that more money will bring happiness . . . when everyone acts on this assumption and incomes generally increase, no one, on the average, feels better off. Yet each person goes on, generation after generation, unaware of the self-defeating process in which he is caught up." The result is one in which economic growth appears to produce more affluence, yet affluence remains illusory and happiness, which is the presumptive goal, is never attained.

In the Declaration of Independence, Jefferson argued for the "pursuit of happiness." For him, liberty was the comprehensive good and happiness one of its outcomes. Happiness, however, was viewed within the constraints of a consensual model of propitious behavior. Surely none of the Founders would have argued for happiness at any price. Happiness was seen as a condition of communal loyalty; in fact, John Locke, sometimes regarded as the philosophical heir of the constitution, employed the word as a substitution for virtue. Happiness does not exempt a son from that honor which he ought to pay his parents; neither does virtue exempt a man from his obligations to a society. Those obligations, if freely chosen, reveal the good and as a consequence unlock the secret of happiness. Presumably, communal virtue represented the legitimate expression of self-interest whose aggregate effect is the common good.

Because virtue was seen as residing in society, governments had to be controlled so that virtue could be protected. In this paradigm, virtue, liberty and happiness are perceived to be in harmony. By allowing liberty, the way is open to live virtuously and as a result to achieve happiness.

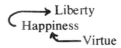

If one accepts this symmetry, the elimination of coercion leads to communal trust.

By contemporary standards, this paradigm seems faulty. Ruthlessness has metastasized throughout the society as growing numbers of individuals assert themselves for personal gain without any regard to the goals of the social order as a whole. As a result, the happiness once defined through liberty and virtue is now cut free from the very values and context that gave it meaning.

Where does that leave us? Drifting in a sea of existential feelings, the average person doesn't know to which shore he can turn for refuge. His search for happiness is made desperate as his need for it increases. But he is in a quandary over how it can be reached. Instead of redirecting his search to the values in his past, modern man metaphorically accelerates his aimless pursuit for "the happy life" only to find it remains beyond his grasp.

Chapter 3

The Myth of Success

"Success has ruined many a man."

Benjamin Franklin

"Success—'that bitch goddess, Success,' in William James'
phrase—demands strange sacrifices from those who worship her."

Aldous Huxley

Several years ago Norman Podhoretz, the editor of
Commentary, wrote a book entitled *Making It.* The story, which
was largely autobiographical, tells the odyssey of a young man
who wants to gain acceptance from the New York literati. His
guile, perseverence and occasionally dissimulation are described
in vivid detail. There was no question in this case that the end was
clearly focused and justified by the means. For many critics the
actions were unconscionable, another literary Sammy Glick.
Others asked "why all the fuss?" And still others maintained
that "success" had changed so substantially that Podhoretz's
goal was simply a chimera.

What this book and its reception represent, I be-
lieve, is more than a simple tale of someone on the make. Nor is it
unusual because it occurs in the allegedly placid world of writers.

17

The books' real contribution — it seemed to me — is its definition of success in contemporary life.

Success in America has had several incarnations. In *The Protestant Ethic and The Spirit of Capitalism* Max Weber argued that in the sixteenth and seventeenth centuries many western Europeans began to accept economic pursuits as ends in themselves. Work was a justification for living; one didn't live only to work. Economic activity joined the spirit of reason to create a uniquely rational system. This system became the "spirit of capitalism" as we understand it. He also noted that in religious maxims prevalent during that period, particularly monasticism, were the virtues of self-control and industry that promoted the growth of capitalism. Presumably, the callings that God assigned to people were to be performed with the same commitment as one would serve God himself. In this scheme each person, whether he be farmer, lawyer or businessman, had a devotional responsibility to his job. A resignation based on God's will had to be accompanied by fervent performance of duty. In this way a monastic self-control was transferred to all economic activity and, more importantly, an ethical impulse became the rationale for capital development.

By subjecting life to a rational discipline, work, diligence, and frugality became economic and ethical norms of conduct at the same time. Moreover, this rational cosmology permitted a definition of success that encompassed these norms. Individual achievement was moderated by the parameters of essentially ascetic, monastic codes. Doing well meant acting in conformity with God's will. For the individual in this system the excesses of vanity could not be evidenced nor, for that matter, could one observe individual ambition for the self which later became the hallmark of capitalism. This monastic order encouraged control, stability and conformity.

For Benjamin Franklin the virtue imposed by providential authority translated into the good life, a view of individual and communal fulfillment. It is instructive that this conception in American life has not been entirely lost. Frank Capra's "It's A Wonderful Life" portrays a character who suppresses personal fulfillment for the welfare of others. While he (Jimmy Stewart) laments this decision he ultimately comes to the realization through God's agent — a guardian angel — that sacrifice for others does lead to the "good life." At the end Stewart recognizes his success when neighbors he has helped in the past come to his aid during a time of personal trial.

During the Jacksonian period symbolic efforts to

democratize the nation took the form of unleashing the control and stability of earlier periods. While virtue and duty were still associated with one's employment there emerged a positive expression of individualism different from the view that individual ambition was necessarily a function of selfishness.

Every man could find his own level in a world of democratic virtue. It is interesting, and obviously related, that the Transcendental Movement germinates from the democratic spirit in the Zeitgeist. To satisfy a dynamic culture which emphasized self reliance, religions concerned themselves with an Arminian belief that God, and as a consequence the power to achieve salvation, is within each of us. No longer is salvation solely a function of good work; it is as the evangelical spirit would have it — in one's self. In its most extreme form this view led to the Antinomian contention that signs of salvation can be obtained on the spot, in the church that releases a deeply spiritual response.

Success may be related to civic duty, but it is also related to an individualistic interpretation of God and his mysterious ways. The moralism associated with good deeds didn't change during the thirty years before the Civil War, but the seeds for a philosophy of individual enterprise were planted in the Unitarian and evangelical churches of that period.

With the rise of industry a vision of money-making dominated the culture. Individualism was transmogrified into an aggressive extension of laissez-faire economics. Self-help counselors felt obliged to distinguish between wealth and worth. While "the man on the make" was not an ideal, there was no question that the lust for money intruded on the expectations of virtue that characterized business in the past. Assurances of opportunity quite naturally became confused with an ambition for wealth. It was also apparent in this gilded age that wealth was seemingly achieved overnight, it conferred social distinction and it was coveted above almost everything else.

While moralists bemoaned the fate of a nation that had lost its ethical bearings, there were visible examples of the super rich who flaunted their anti-religious sentiments. Cynics maintained that even the wealthy reputed to be religious prayed on Sunday but preyed on people the other six days of the week. "Mercantile degeneracy" was a common expression of the period, but it did not deter the ambitious from pursuing the goal of wealth with an unswerving loyalty. Eventually, the moralists conceded by suggesting that virtuous behavior is *more likely* to assure success than immoral behavior. To those who were unsuccessful this was small consolation. In a society where the myth of success was achieved with wealth, competitors refused to look back; their eyes were peeled on the goal line and neither religious tradition nor contemporary morality could slow them down.

There is no question that the Horatio Alger novels and other inspirational books had a large market during the late nineteenth century. But the impact of these books had to be appreciated against a backdrop of industrialization, rapid social mobility and unprecedented urbanization. In fact, despite the obvious virtue of Alger's leading character, it was easy to identify his success with worship of the dollar. Far from condemning Mammon, most of the inspirational authors and many contemporary muckrakers accepted "the bitch goddess" as the indispensable feature of American life.

In the scramble for wealth, some areas of virtuous behavior gradually became a casualty. Venality and worldly rewards had become so closely associated in the public's view by the twentieth century that the original Christian idea for capital accumulation had seemingly been turned upside down. It was replaced by the newly popularized dogma of social Darwinism. Gobineau, Spencer, and Madison Grant were undoubtedly alien names to the panjandrum of industry, but their ideas became a useful rationalization for some of the unseemly consequences of rapid development. William Graham Sumner's plea to "root, hog or die" served to legitimate a laissez-faire acceptance of the economic order; it also served to justify a particular perception of success.

The twentieth century was accompanied by the propagandized Marxist assumption that industry protected itself and damned the rest. An acceptance of individual responsibility for success turned into a belief that diminished opportunity was a collective responsibility. This mythology didn't replace the old one completely, nor is the struggle resolved, but the direction became clear. With the necessary support — suggests the presumption of the "new social psychology" — *every individual is entitled* to some degree of success. A philosophy of rags to riches has been replaced by a spirit of universal access to wealth.

In part the power of psychology supported this mystique. People like Mary Baker Eddy, Dale Carnegie and Norman Vincent Peale borrowed from Freud and the Transcendentalists to argue that since people are endowed with constructive desires and since God is within each of us, an ethic of "positive thinking" can be created which releases our self possessed power for success. This psychology of success dichotomized into conservative and liberal schools. The former argued that since the power for success is within each of us the external support of government is unnecessary. The latter maintains that the inherent constructive power cannot be released without the assistance of government aid that provides the minimal economic basis for self respect.

As success became increasingly widespread, the psychology that supports the mystique has produced its own nemesis. Due in large part to the popular interpretations of Abraham Maslow, a school of psychology euphemistically called the Human Potential Movement has disseminated the belief that material success is on the low end of a hierarchy of needs and should not be pursued as avidly as self-fulfillment (an expression that vaguely suggests self improvement). Of course one has to have enough of the material success to reject it. And one most certainly must have enough money to support a guru who says that money isn't worth the effort involved in getting it.

It is ironic that many of those with wealth have returned to the monastic ideal that success is a function of pursuing one's religious conviction. And those without wealth argue that either the government should open the door to success or by dint of personal effort they will achieve the still worthwhile goal on their own. The middle class, in other words the bulk of the population, is confused. Media presentations describe the good life as one of material things, yet the examples of those with obvious success who reject it all do not go unnoticed. In a significant sense this population is trapped by competing myths. On the one hand, is the tradition of hard work and self control that translates into financial rewards and on the other is the rejection of a crude materialism that cannot be a measure of one's self-worth or provide a true measure of success.

Perhaps what confuses many of us is the non-material dimensions of success. If one can't have the kind of wealth that kindles a sense of importance, then importance may be generated out of images which suggest success. In his analysis of images in America, Daniel Boorstin argued that we have created for ourselves "a self-deceiving magic of prestige" in which impressions are everything. In fact, as Boorstin put it, the contrivance is so commonplace that the genuine begins to appear artificial. Leaders of business are not simply executives; they are policy-makers. Mechanics don't simply fix our cars; they are mechanical experts who investigate engine dysfunction. We don't have problems that are discussed with friends; we have blocks that are explored with therapists. We don't do a job; we change the course of events. We don't plan a vacation with a travel agent; we seek a unique experience with a travel expert. We don't live our lives; we seek adventures. We have become a population of Muhammed Alis shouting "I am the greatest" in an attempt to prove to ourselves that we are successful.

Yet, the illusion so dominates the actual that our expectations of success are not satisfied by what we do and what material and psychic rewards we receive. Success becomes ever more elusive because it changes as we reach new plateaus. Our age might be described with P. T. Barnum's expression "promise almost everything for next to nothing." Increase the expectations of success even if the substance of those expectations is bogus. Is the sanitary engineer really different from the garbage man? And confuse the actual differences by making the synthetic seem real. Take our celebrities and describe them as heroes. Degrade all fame into notoriety. Make Farrah Fawcett-Majors a heroine and Robert Redford a notable American. In the process what we observe as the goal of success is undermined by an illusion that can never be satisfied and can only be addressed with illusory and counterfeit solutions.

What our culture very often interprets as success is a name, a name that is known. It makes little difference how one's name is presented in the media as long as it is presented and spelled accurately. One component of this emphasis on notoriety is the award game. There are so many awards given for so many trivial accomplishments that it is difficult to be a celebrity without winning one. Television's big events can be described as one award ceremony after another.

For the anonymous person there are also "awards without meaning." Every bowler gets a trophy even if he averages 150 a game. Every golfer gets an award: "the best golfer with a 35 handicap." Basketball teams get awards for being winners in the runner-up division. And students are given grades as awards, an "A" for doing the best mediocre paper. Excellence isn't awarded, because we have lost sight of what that is. Every university is described as great. Every student is depicted as having talent. And every media event is portrayed as bigger and better than the last one. The concern, at the moment, is to democratize success; actually to so rob it of its meaning by giving it to everyone that discriminating between successful and unsuccessful is impossible.

If everyone can appear to be successful, what does success mean? If the myth of success is debunked, what is left to strive for? Andy Warhol argued — quite rightly — that in a television age everyone can be king for a day. Is it exaggerated to argue that the average secretary in America has traveled more than the richest person in the world one hundred years ago? This — I might add — isn't a snobbish denunciation of technical accomplishments; but it is an explanation of the difficulty involved in interpreting success at a time when it is seemingly extended without distinction.

Why all the fuss? you ask. Is the confusion and democratization of success so bad? What ails us—as I see it—is that a myth of hard work has been replaced by a myth of consumption and illusion. Our wants have out-stripped our gives and our system is in serious trouble of being unable to satisfy universal desire. More importantly we suffer from our illusions. We have so deluded ourselves with a masquerade of success that we are often unable to distinguish between the genuinely worthwhile and the inadequate replicas.

It is not enough to dispel the ghosts, we should once again consider the nature of our real successes. Perhaps this means — in part — resurrecting the early success myth so that positive images and actual accomplishments might be nourished. We are all aware of gigantic future problems of taxation, finance, and development. But the recent past has been so euphoric and pleasant that it seems almost subversive to worry about the future. We have arrived at almost national success, even if the meaning of success isn't clear anymore. If the future is bleak so be it, the comforts of the present are heady. Yet our comforts derive in part from the residual effect of the Horatio Alger myth of hard work, decency, and commensurate rewards, and that myth is almost gone.

It is obviously regarded as an empty cliche in our time of cynicism, but Luke Larkin, one of Horatio Alger's characters, who struggled from boyhood privation and self denial into a manhood of prosperity and honor, may not be an inappropriate myth for our future. As Horatio Alger maintained, "There has been some luck about it, I admit, but after all he (Luke Larkin) is indebted for most of his good fortune to his own good qualities." Are there many people in our time who can make such a claim?

Chapter 4

The Myth of Equality

"That all men are equal is a proposition to which, at ordinary times, no sane individual has ever given his assent."

Aldous Huxley

In the 1920's several interpreters of Darwinian thought asked why should some contestants have an insurmountable headstart in a metaphorical race for survival. Lester Ward responded with suggestions that government agencies assist those with handicaps so that the starting line is approximately the same for everyone. For half a century that has been a conventional wisdom. But that is about to change. Now it is contended by John Rawls and his devotees that the starting line is less significant than the finishing line. It isn't enough to handicap the race he argues; the society has an obligation to make sure that everyone finishes and, more significantly, that everyone finishes in a dead heat.

If the earlier Darwinians were handicappers, the Rawlsians are fixers. Equality of opportunity has been replaced by equality of result. And government not only assists in making the race fair, it monitors the speed and the finish to ensure the desired results.

Equality is one of the great conjuring terms of our age. It is invoked by every social analyst, but its meaning varies from one to another. Either equality is a realizable goal of shared sensibilities or it is an abstraction of idealistic concerns. Some maintain that the goal of equality stands as a guidepost from which we explain and justify unequal outcomes and disparities in income and status. According to this position, the paucity of "alpha" positions forces most people to face the gap between aspirations and achievement. The consequence is an impression of failure or, at the very least, self-doubt. To compensate for these impressions a counterfeit world of success is invented: inflated titles for mundane jobs; investing our children with our aspirations; creating material symbols of success, e.g. big cars; a school of psychoanalysis which suggests "I'm okay"; and a snobbery towards those who have failed more than the rest of us.

If one accepts this position, both the inventions of success and the actual examples of failure are necessary to sustain our fragile egos. Even our social programs aimed at assisting the downtrodden are — according to this logic — symbols of the glaring inequalities that bolster a sense of "our" privilege and "their" lack of success. What emerges from this analysis — perhaps what emerges from all analyses which emphasize equality over individuality — is an economy of collective welfare as the "good society." It is interesting that very few social analysts adopting this argument see the potential damage to individual will. Their conception — like Edward Bellamy's in *Looking Backward* — is based on the unproven (unprovable?) assumption that people gain self-esteem *primarily* from contributions to the commonweal. Instead of suppressing natural instincts of individual will, this society of equality unlocks the true desire for charity and altruism; a passion consistent with individual ambition and initiative.

The presumption in this intoxicating analysis is that a cultural myth over which we have no control has enveloped us. Institutions determine our lot and our belief in the individual as central to the culture becomes a fiction. Inventions — designed by governmental instrumentalities — exist to justify an equality that is intrinsic to this structure. The myth eventually leaves no room for alternative values or individual will with which to counteract the insidious grip of an expanding public sector.

This analysis, which might be described as radical, perhaps even Marxist, has the superficial virtue of giving lip service to a passionate humanitarianism. It defines the natural instincts of people as charitable; it divorces inequality from human intention and it makes the simple argument that "if you can send a man to the moon, we can eliminate inequality."

Yet, it is precisely because this position is so simple, unequivocal and imbued with goodness that it is so wrong-headed. Most people do not easily fit the procrustean models of social scientists. Their views reflect the complexity of life. What most people can experience, many social scientists cannot analyze. For example, however much many people underestimate the obstacles facing the poor, they do see the underprivileged as having some measure of responsibility for their plight. Suffering from the flaw of "aggregate logic," some social analysts, on the other hand, are convinced that if success and failure *are not entirely* related to individual will, they are perforce related to the social structure. This is something like arguing that every deflowered woman who has lost her virginity is a whore. The organization of our culture is much less ordered and intentional, much more fraught with ambiguity than the melodramatic expression of the radical social analysts would have us believe.

Yet, suppose the dream of a social system based on equality were to emerge. What evolution could one envision short of the completely managed society that removes individual rewards for recognized achievement? Either achievement would be seen differently (read: compatible with the government standards) or rewards would be unrelated to achievement. This is a hypothetical possibility unsubstantiated by empirical evidence. But the model inevitably depends on a government supported mythology that promotes the idea of personal sacrifice for the state. In any scenario of this condition, management of achievement, however unobtrusive, would have to be sustained by government officials. It seems to me that the result of this system is not a life of "all sweet and no bitter" as Lucy of *Peanuts* fame demanded; but the substitution of arsenic for sugar (they both may kill, yet who would prefer death by poison to obesity?).

Actually, equality is a word masquerading as a protest ideal. It is an attempt to adjudicate the difference between the sexes; it represents the principle of treating people in roughly the same way before the law; it permits a multitude of religious expressions; it encourages opportunity; it recognizes political rights and it even supports self-esteem. What it does not do is redistribute wealth to satisfy an abstract ideal of economic parity. The American ideal, to the extent it is discernible at all, has been hypocritical on the matter of equality. We give lip service to egalitarian principles, but act in a way that denotes individual distinctions. This disharmony between principle and action has not resulted in disruption because we have simply chosen to identify equality with individual rights, a definition that is handy and utilitarian. My contention is not cynical. Since the abstract goal of equality — in the sense that all people will be the same — is not achievable, it makes sense to mollify the protest impulses with stated principles and act in accordance with common sense.

It is also obvious, I believe, that the relationship between success and equality is generally misunderstood by orthodox egalitarians. As a kid growing up in a family of very modest means there was never any talk about invidious comparisons with people who owned chauffeur driven limousines or even those who could afford second homes in the country. The comparisons were with our neighbors next door who were as poor as we were. What I found extraordinary was the ability of the Schwartz's next door to buy a television set when my folks had difficulty paying the rent. Success for me was being able to have a family television set; it had nothing to do with Madison Avenue hyperbole or striving to be like the Jones' on Park Avenue. Simply put, ordinary folks measure their success and equality by their relative position to other ordinary folks. The idea that the average man is discouraged when he compares himself to Nelson Rockefeller is a pernicious myth that can easily be dispelled by any half hour spent in a truckers bar in Queens listening to the conversation.

What is rather startling to me is that those who advocate equality of results don't seem to be talking to average people. Of course this is not surprising. In the name of the average man and woman, the Populists have maintained that one can infer unequal opportunity from unequal results. If one accepts this logic then the annual thrashing Penn State gives Syracuse on the football field is not due to its talented football players but rules that must have been rigged to ensure the result. In this case the assumption of equality extrapolates into the equal distribution of results. It seems to me worth recalling John C. Calhoun's argument that inequality of condition is the natural product of equality of opportunity. If everyone has the opportunity to play the game the good players are more likely to win than the average or bad ones. In schoolyards all over America this is axiomatic.

In the last two decades this issue has been accentuated by the continual expansion of rights and opportunities. One could make the claim that in the last half century there has been an evolution of privileges that have become demands, demands that have become rights and rights that have finally emerged as entitlements. Yet a war on poverty, affirmative action struggles, welfare rights demonstrations have not redistributed wealth. What most people know intuitively is what government officials are beginning to discover: Equal opportunity cannot guarantee equal outcomes. Since an inverse correlation probably does exist between these values, advocates of equal opportunity and equal outcomes will have to resolve their differences in a political struggle. That struggle may very well bring down the mythic structure that permitted a congruence of individual will and egalitarian standards for two hundred years. But it will not equalize things. As long as human traits are distributed along "the tyranny of the bell-shaped curve" — to borrow a phrase from Irving Kristol — all the maneuvering and spending and taxing is not going to make human conditions equal.

Many of the exercises designed to equalize the system challenge the Aristotelian assumption that inequality can be a catalyst for the common good. Clearly, poverty has produced an Al Capone, but it has also produced Abraham Lincoln. The incentive for "getting ahead" has always been inequality. Our present reformers, however, wish to equalize the population by making the successful less successful enough so that their descent meets the ascent of the rising poor. In a real sense the progressive income tax is a definition of this theory. By becoming more successful, one not only pays more but the rate of taxation increases. Demonstrating one's relative strength in the marketplace is cause for the punitive whip of increased taxes. What other explanation is there for this obviously unfair arrangement except imposed equality? Surely, a fixed tax percentage would lead to more taxes as one's income increased. But our system is intentionally progressive because it responds to the vengeful need "to soak the rich." With inflation now driving the average man's salary superficially high, it is difficult to tell whether the tax system soaks the rich or drenches everyone. And who, I might ask, is the beneficiary of this arrangement? The poor do not perceive their condition as improved through tax levied government programs and the most productive sectors of the society develop a disincentive for productive work when the government is a full partner in all income earned.

Why — one may naturally ask — do many retain faith in the idea of equality when policies designed to achieve the goal are so patently unfair? It seems to me that without exhausting the range of explanations, there are four compelling reasons for their adoption. First, is the obvious conflict between the new class (the professionals and technocrats) and the bourgeoisie. This conflict takes place on many fronts. From the point of view of the new class the struggle is intended to reflect an anti-business ethos and a distaste for the bourgeois cultural standards associated with the Protestant ethic. The seeming desire for equality is less an ideal and more a protest. In the last two decades the nation has witnessed dramatic improvement in the bottom quartile of the population at the expense of the top quartile, thereby compressing the statistical differences between wage earners. Yet, the dissatisfaction of the new class has increased. Irving Kristol has contended that the new class doesn't want equality; it is seeking power. If this is true — as I suspect it to be — the call for egalitarian standards really means equality for you and superiority for me.

Second, is the widely held populist assumption that the rich are less moral than the rest of us and, as a consequence, obtained their wealth from illicit activity. The desire to equalize becomes "a valid" effort to punish the wealthy for their evil ways. It is curious, however, that wealth is defined selectively. Only business wealth is considered evil. Mick Jagger, Kareem Abdul Jabbar, Dr. J, the Bee Gees are shielded from the assaults leveled against corporate leaders.

Third, comes the contention that an equal distribution of wealth and rights will stabilize the society. Presumably, satisfaction will emerge when everyone believes that equal treatment leads to equal outcomes. Once again the evidence betrays the dream. The more nearly equal people are the more they exaggerate the petty differences between themselves. I offer that statement without reservations because I am so confident about its veracity. The drive to free the spirit of individual will leads inevitably to the declaration that "I am unique." Unless the spirit is completely repressed (the Skinnerian models in the Soviet Union and China make me pause), pure equality is an unrealizable goal. Even if it were realizable, is the goal more significant than the price that would have to be paid in sacrificing liberty and fairness?

Last, is the Christopher Jencks argument that since success is related "to varieties of luck and on-the-job competence," the government should attempt to reduce the rewards of success through even more progressive taxes and attempts to mitigate the effects of failure. This argument, which relies on the premise that inequality is a throw of the dice, moves with giant leaps of faith to the conclusion that "egalitarianism is simply another way of saying that we think need should play a larger role than it now does in determining what people get back from society." But what in this calculus do we mean by "larger?" Who makes the decisions about need? And, how do we encourage incentives for production when the more one earns the more tax he pays? The answer to these questions is the belief that popular assumptions about rewards "can be altered by deliberate efforts of the state . . ." Once again the socialist panacea rears its head as the way to improve the condition of the poor and as an instrument for making those with high incomes "begin to feel ashamed of economic inequality." But, as George McGovern, among others has learned, those who have high incomes and those with low incomes are not easy to determine. And even if one could — using some arbitrary cut off point — the result would not lead to the intended equality.

If one were to employ the Jencks' argument as a metaphor for sports, there would be a random selection of athletes for the starting team so that the rewards of success were not exaggerated and some would not be forced to feel the pangs of failure. The only problem is that the game won't be worth watching and won't even be worth playing. Some marginal and poor players may be content, but the level of play will reach the lowest common denominator of talent. What may emerge is a homogeneous standard of performance that will make the game insipid. Notwithstanding the emotional costs of inequality which the adversary culture exaggerates, any game, including the game of life, has reduced benefits without a standard of excellence. And excellence is a function of incentive. To reduce incentive is to reduce all human enterprise to the mean. Can you imagine what basketball would be without Dr. J or football without O.J.? Can you imagine a computer making random decisions about who plays? The result would be reminiscent of the incident in *Gulliver's Travels* when the tailors in the kingdom of La Puta make a suit of clothes for the hero by very elaborate and precise mechanical means; and, which when worn, turns out to be ill-fitting. The schemes for equality are very much like this. Our government will devise elaborate means for the introduction of egalitarian standards. It will employ computers, determine what is a fair wage and how "need" would be satisfied. In the end, however, it will all be as ill-fitting as Gulliver's clothes.

Chapter 5

Myth of Technology

"No machine will increase the possibilities of life."
John Ruskin

"Faith in machinery is our besetting danger; often in machinery most absurdly disproportioned to the end which this machinery if it is to do any good at all, is to serve; but always in machinery, as if it had a value in and for itself."
Matthew Arnold

There is no event that has shaped the character of this century as much as the introduction of technology. We are at a point in historical evolution when the myth of Daedalus is upon us. Machines, it has been argued save us from ourselves. They are, contends Michael Harrington, the new slaves in a new world, a world in which personal fulfillment can be achieved as never before. Aristotle wrote, with extraordinary prescience: "There is only one condition in which we can imagine managers not needing subordinates, and masters not needing slaves. This condition would be that each (inanimate) instrument could do its own work, at the word of command or by intelligent anticipation, like the statues of Daedalus . . ."

When Descartes described "the ghost in the machine," he was arguing metaphorically for the mind-body dichotomy. However, the ghost in the contemporary machine is the anthropomorphic quality we've attributed to technology. The prevailing belief that technology possesses Zeus-like powers to solve our woe, eliminate poverty and make us feel better about ourselves may well be the reason for our social malaise. Our expectations cannot be satisfied by the reality of technological achievement.

We are told that if we brush with one toothpaste as opposed to another, we'll have a better sex life. If we dress in fashionable clothes, we'll get better jobs. If we use the right deodorant, we'll be loved by our family. If we drive a sporty car, we'll have sex appeal. If we wash with the appropriate soap, we'll have the glow of youth. Yet, after we've washed, brushed, dressed, sprayed and driven with the right product we find that we are no younger, no more sexy and no more desirable than we were before. The promise of the good life through the world of technology is bogus. It isn't that technology can't deliver a fine car or a good soap. It can and does. The problem is we have so exaggerated the consequences of technology's products that it is impossible for our expectations to be realized. For many, the result is anguish. Having played the roles prescribed by the advertisers many find that their lives are still empty and the gifts of technology do not correspond to the world of illusions.

In a way the gifts of technology are decisive in what we are and how we see ourselves. Our reference point to other people is frequently what T. S. Eliot called the "objective correlative". In the tradition of establishing a mastery over nature through the world of science and technology, we undermined transcendence and joined forces with the Faustians. In Beverly Hills the car you buy is considered a function of your personality. The car is to that culture what predestination was to the Puritans. It determines where you go to school, who your friends will be, what attitudes you'll have, and what will be written in your obituary.

What the widespread introduction of technology has produced is the exact opposite of scientific intention. Historically, the philosophers of science sought an expression of man's power in coping with nature. Yet ironically technology is often perceived as eluding man's will. It seemingly has a life and direction of its own beyond our understanding and control. Jacques

Ellul writes: "Technique exists because it is technique. The golden age will be because it will be. Any other answer is superfluous."

A myth of technological impotence has emerged from the impression that there are technological forces at work that have a momentum of their own and on which we are dependent for even the barest necessities. Even our language is influenced by the context of technological achievements. Information is "input" and connection is "interface." We are all programmers of the future using the technical nervous system that has — in many quarters — replaced providential will.

In "2001: A Space Odyssey" Stanley Kubrick presents a wonderfully illustrative moment of technological impotence. H.A.L., the computer on board the space craft, malfunctions, taking on totalitarian qualities alien to the original computer program. The astronauts are helpless at first. Faced with the Hobson's choice of working with a totalitarian computer on which their life support system depends or destroying it, they opt for the latter. But the degree to which they are dependent on technology and helpless in the face of a computer "gone mad" is an appropriate metaphor for the society's present dilemma.

The myth of technology has created the illusion that anything is possible, even our collective salvation; but it has also increased our reliance on machines, and, as a consequence, dehumanized our relations with other people. In a significant way we have let technology become our will. We rely on technology for the problems we can't solve and when we don't like the solutions, we simply describe the program as unsatisfactory or the machines as inadequate. The problem is never diagnosed in ourselves. This situation is analogous to the addict who blames drugs for his addiction. It is true, of course, that the drugs are addicting, but in attributing powers of control to the chemicals, the addict has surrendered an ability to assert his will. He argues implicitly that the addiction absolves him from exercising his judgement. Yet, the drug itself is neutral; it is not the drug which is responsible for addiction, but the addict.

Machines are like drugs. We may increase our reliance on them, attribute grand powers to them, but in the end they are only an extension of ourselves. Our technology may be able to produce the test tube fetus, but it cannot tell us whether life created in this way is desirable. The machine has made it easier to transmit information, yet it is increasingly more difficult to sort out the trivial from the important. In its way technology has forced us to examine the human dimensions of our decisions at the moment we seem reluctant to accept the responsibility.

We are instructed by the media everyday that there is no aspect of our lives that can't be improved through the use of technology's products. But the improvement, when it occurs, is never enough. Raising the material level of millions of people beyond any expectation of the past is, indeed, the singular accomplishment of technology in the century. Yet, happiness does not abound. On the contrary, the search for happiness is more desperate because our technological gods have seemingly failed us. We want to turn on our lives the way in which technology allows us to turn on our television sets. But life is not technology and all those psychic cures that simulate technology's methods inevitably end in disappointment. So, after you've decided input equals output; after you've been Ested and analyzed, had your ego massaged and your back Rolffed, you are still the same person searching for answers to a world made treacherous by the erosion of traditions. Technology can't help, nor can the techniques of psychology that ignore the fundamental questions of existence.

Notwithstanding its lack of will, technology does have a compelling mystique. It captivates our imagination to believe the machines are like the genie trapped in a bottle to be exploited at command. Even if it is not true — as Charlie Chaplin in "Modern Times" discovers — our interest isn't thwarted. A World's Fair enthralls us because, like the children staring at the toys in an F.A.O. Schwarz display window, we can observe at first hand the miracles machines can produce. But there is another side to this picture.

The mystique of technology is related to its sheer power, to its potential as devices for war. In technology can be found the ultimate weapons, presumably those devices that can determine the future of the globe. On the one hand, the destructive capacity of the weapons creates a balance of terror, a balance sustained by the mutual fear of deployment. Ferlinghetti once wrote that it was possible to love the bomb because its very existence in two distinct ideological worlds precludes its uses. However, it can also be argued that the result of a hypothetical strategic war based on first, second and third strike capabilities has real political implications. The seriousness of sabre rattling is determined by the credibility of strategic weapon strength. If the United States did not have superior missile strength in 1962, its verbal efforts to deter the Soviet missile plans in Cuba would not have worked. In fact, one could easily conclude that our inability to deter the Russians in Ethiopia, Angola, Afghanistan, South Yemen, and Iran is due to the fact that our missile superiority has been lost.

Note that the theoretical notions of missile strength have practical political results. No one knows for sure what the result of a nuclear exchange would be. Yet, with the exception of the psychopaths, no one wants to find out. Therefore, arms accumulation is not a fatuous exercise but a political necessity. To exercise our will we must demonstrate our strength. The conjectural and the real converge on the blackboard of strategic planners. One could make the logical assumption that the discovery of a laser that can destroy all surveillance satellites and all missile silos and submarines would so upset the balance of power that not a shot would need to be fired to gain global control.

In the narrow sense technology may be seen as an instrument for power. But it is still separate from will. Of course, with no strength the constraints of reality impinge on will. It is through will that man's intervention in technological development will make a difference. It is only human will that can overcome the myth of technology, a myth that at once hypnotizes us with possibilities while letting us down with the despair of unfulfilled expectations.

William James argued that when a mountain climber finds himself in a situation where he has to jump across an abyss to save himself and believes he can do it, he is much more likely to succeed than if he doubts his belief. Believing he can do it, the climber bolsters his energies by means of his faith. When he reaches the other side of the peak, his belief will have been confirmed.

Believing that we can control the tools of technology is more than half way to actually doing it. We may demythologize technology by emphasizing man's role in its creation and, simultaneously, man's capacity for controlling it. The computer, for example, is a mirror of our systems; it merely records what is observable but it cannot possibly affect the causes of despair and joy. It cannot possibly homogenize human emotions so that one answer is true for everyone. Its potential for growth is limited by our potential to unlock the mysteries of learning. And our potential is trapped by the unsolved riddles of our evolutionary history.

The dialectic of technology claims that inanimate objects can cause us to consider the most fundamental questions of life because the material things that technology produces leave us with a desire for spiritual fulfillment. The mystique of technological power has left us powerless seeking as rarely before an answer to our Being. Jacques Ellul has written, "There is no hope, and the dream is no longer the personal act of an individual who freely chooses to flee some 'reality' or other. It is a mass phenomenon of millions of men who desire to help themselves to a slice of life, freedom, and immortality. Separated from his essence, like a snail deprived of its shell, man is only a blob of plastic matter modeled after the moving images."

Is this true? Is this the inexorable direction of technological development? In the 17th century, Hobbes contended that life was "nasty, brutish, and short." One could argue that, due to technology, life is now long, comfortable, and meaningless. Meanwhile, how is meaning introduced into the life of comfort? The answer is already obvious: It is seen in the despair of those who have all that can possibly be consumed, yet remain dissatisfied. It is observable in a frantic search for recognition that is widely heralded as the era of narcissism. It is found in the fatuous behavior of disco kings and queens who are burned out at 30. Since meaning is not found in the superficial delights of life, something else must be found: a transcendence. The belief that we are only part of a grand design puts our humanity in an appropriate perspective. Even if one accepts the notion that God does not exist, still divinity must be sought. Man must seek beyond himself to find his true self. That path is the way of faith. There is no other answer; certainly it is not to be found in the myth of technology. The French poet Paul Valery maintained, "There is only one thing to do — to redo oneself." It is none too soon for this action. Even if we are not sure of what we believe, we can still practice the exercise of faith. As Isaac Bashevis Singer reminds us, in the act of continual prayer one's faith increases.

Chapter 6

Myth of Small Is Beautiful

> "I have seen enlightened management and foolish management in both large companies and small. The difference has been not in the size or structure of the organization but in the qualities of the men who run it."
>
> Robert Stein

It is often maintained that beauty is in the eye of the beholder. Presumably, if one accepts this old chestnut, beauty could be found in the mammoth pyramids and in the diminutive wood cuts of Durer. In fact, one could argue there is no correlation between beauty and size. One could make that argument, but today it is not very likely one will.

A popular myth that owes a great deal to E. F. Schumacher — "small is beautiful" — or its counterpart often attributed to Kingsley Amis that "more is worse," has captured the imagination of the media and, I suspect, of the youth market as totally as rock music or astrology tables.

It may be true that some institutions must somehow diminish in size in order to provide adequate service with limited resources. But it doesn't follow that this is true of all or most institutions. The city, for example, cannot have meaning without "bigness." Without it there is unlikely to be diversity and without diversity there are limits to individual expression and experimentation, the very values that give cities their vitality. The positive values one normally associates with the city — tolerance, innovation, enthusiasm, nonconformity — are products of city life precisely because of the large and shifting populations in metropolitan areas.

It is absurd to accept *a priori* the idea that "more is worse" without realizing why growth is necessary, or without calculating the amount of growth that is desirable. Those anti-urban lobbyists, who argue for the dismantling of our cities, have already reached the conclusion that cities will be habitable only if they are smaller than they are at present.

In fairness to Schumacher, — who Governor Jerry Brown once described as his guru, it should be pointed out that he acknowledges the need for appropriate scale depending on the requirements of the activity. But in decrying the "idolatry of giantism," he has nonetheless inspired an idolatry of the diminutive. It is probably self-evident that more money will not guarantee the solution to most of our problems. But it is not clear that more money won't — in many instances — help. It is probably true that adding another layer of bureaucracy in most government agencies will not provide a productive change. Yet, it is not clear that if this layer were populated by extremely talented people, they would not have a salutary effect on the specific organization. More could be worse and, indeed, may be worse, but there are too many examples to the contrary to make the claim axiomatic. Yet, this pernicious myth persists with relatively few challenges, even when its effects are adverse.

As David Potter has argued in *People of Plenty,* America never really had to face the choice of an egalitarian or individualistic cosmology because our natural abundance allowed us to evade the issue. American history has not been characterized by the expropriation from some and the aggrandizement of others. In America it was simply assumed that through growth, the economic position of all parties would improve, even if that wealth were disproportionately distributed. By drawing on nature's bounty and on technological development, America has dealt with the problem of social reform without exacerbating the natural tensions between classes.

But if we suppose — as the disciples of Schumacher insist — that nature's resources are not bounteous, that scientists and engineers are not infinitely ingenious, and that "zero growth," as E. J. Mishan has argued, is desirable, then the hostility between equality and individualism will be so sharpened that class conflict is inevitable.

David Donald, the American historian, has argued that this is already happening. The energy problem is only the tip of the iceberg. According to Donald, America's future will be accompanied by social commotion because we have restricted our goals. In substituting a philosophy of scarcity for a philosophy of abundance, it is natural to expect the competition between groups to increase. As the Bakke case suggests, our society is deeply divided over the question of whether status can be divorced from performance; whether achievement may be overlooked in the quest for equality. As groups compete vigorously for a share of a smaller or stable proverbial pie, the method of distribution becomes ever more questionable, ever more difficult to justify. What has emerged in the current debate over economic "fairness" is the underlying principle of equality that had been glossed over for so long: Equality has in substantial measure been a function of abundance. To accept the position that small is better runs counter to the operating, albeit concealed, assumption of American economic and political life.

Is the s-i-b position justified? Is it true that America has reached a stage of development in which further growth is unnecessary, perhaps even dangerous? There are no simple answers to these questions. Surely, the concern over environmental damage is greater today than at the time when serious environmental damage actually did occur. It is also true that primary manufacturing tasks have given way to managerial work. Moreover, American products have difficulty competing with foreign competitors and, when one controls for inflation, the growth rate of the G.N.P. is negligible. There are relatively few growth areas in the economy; yet, like the dark cloud of preshadowed gloom, the reliance on *cheap* foreign oil increases the outflow of American dollars and makes it difficult to generate the capital necessary for industrial expansion. The problems are formidable.

Some critics of the industrial system maintain that if we consume less, reduce our needs, and limit our size that the solution will be in hand. Limited scale, it might be contended, is the variant on which prospects of a bright future can be restored. However, this belief is predicated on the view that what we now have is enough, that any attempt to increase production and size will have serious consequences. Coal production as a substitute for oil, for example, is viewed as a step backward, a contradiction of "clean air standards" adopted by Congress, even though there is more than enough available coal to meet our energy needs. We have so emphasized the quality of life, to use a very popular cliche, that we have subordinated the importance of the quantity or abundance of life. This in part explains why legislators are so obsessed with regulation while tending to ignore the conditions that might produce economic growth. It is interesting that many social analysts dismiss the simple fact that ignoring economic growth is like killing the goose that laid the golden egg. In other words, there can probably be little concern for quality without quantity.

The view that America has become "large enough" is, under careful scrutiny, patently absurd. Much of our nation remains underdeveloped and underpopulated. Too, there is the potential for building new towns and restoring those parts of old cities that can still be saved. There are new sources of energy that can be developed and old sources that can still be found, albeit that requires large investments. And there are still homes to build, clothes to manufacture and needs of every sort to be met. To suggest that America is at a mature stage of development is not to claim that our energies need to be exhausted or our vision proscribed.

Growth is not perforce "wasteful." As obvious as this statement may be, it requires restatement. We have become so inured to Parkinson's Laws that it is natural to associate increased size with waste. "More government is bad government" or "that government is best which rules least" are claims that influence our perception. Of course, they are also true, as far as they go. In some instances additional employees are precisely what is needed to make an organization function well. In some cases government action may lead to a social result that would not occur through inaction. And, while money cannot in itself solve problems, it can sometimes make the difference between a marginally sound versus a very sound institution.

The problem with size — at least to the extent the argument is applied to government — is that it is often confused with strength. But in many institutions the bigger they get the flabbier and fatter they get. Conceivably a big and strong institution would be ideal just as a big and weak one represents an awful model. Big and weak institutions are usually responsible for exaggerated claims based on large size and an inability to deliver what is promised because of weakness. The discontinuity is responsible for a disillusionment which translates into cynicism about any institutional acts. As our society creates bigger institutions that are forced into expressing extreme statements, e.g., "the best car ever made," "the eradication of poverty," yet do not possess the resources to make the claims realities, disbelief crops up as the inevitable response by the citzenry.

Perhaps the most significant disappointment in big government is prompted by the welfare state. Such a state not only promised to provide some social service; it seemed to be the harbinger of the new and happy society. Yet, it was doomed to fail. Despite modest successes in some social areas, the government cannot make people happy, eliminate ugliness, reduce envy, or prevent strife. As Peter Drucker indicated, the best we can expect from the welfare state is a relatively well-operated insurance company. Whether the issue is economics, education, transportation or urban renewal, the hyperbole of welfare-state goals makes even minimal results unlikely. It appears that the more administration there is, the more mismanagement occurs.

This condition, I might add, appears to be global. Incompetence, after all, is not an American monopoly. Problems of misgovernment exist in Britain, Japan, the Soviet Union, and almost anywhere in South America. What is characteristic of our system, however, are the exaggerated and largely unattainable goals assigned government. Even when some results are positive, they are undermined by the expectations. In part, this explains why President Johnson's success in creating the expanded welfare state was unappreciated, while Kennedy's failure to enact similar legislation did him almost no political harm at all.

There are now ten times as many government agencies concerned with urban problems as there were in 1939. There are 170 different federal aid programs financed by over 400 separate appropriations. While much of this activity has a negligible effect, and in some instances a negative effect, the fact is there have been some positive changes. But from a reading of newspapers and viewing of television programs, you wouldn't know it. Sober supporters of welfare statism once recognized limitations. However, many other advocates were drunk with utopian ideology and were believers in the destructive myth that spending more money will *surely* solve social problems.

It seems to me that modern government is ungovernable not because of an independent and inert bureaucracy (albeit that contributes to the problem), but because of political confusion. How can a government that wins public support with its intention of creating needed social programs suggest that the need is not greater than the financial risk in operating the programs? The answer is that it must go into debt or call into question its own legitimacy. In creating the illusion that one can have more for less, government has created the unrealistic: an expectation and, as a result, the notion that malevolence must account for our woe appears like a reasonable explanation of social problems.

Big is not better because our purposes are not clear. It has become easy to assign all blame to expanding bureaucracy. But we forget that bureaucrats deal with procedures, not aims. If the goals aren't clear, they can't be faulted for the results. Or, if the goals are clear but unattainable, they are obviously not to blame for our dissatisfaction with government.

In the long run, having a consistent and realistic policy may be the key to governing effectively. But consistency, like politics, is dependent on an ever more elusive consensus. Clearly, consensus is more likely with two people than one hundred, but it is not guaranteed. Any government that avoids the complete dictates of totalitarian rule — whether it be Nauru or the United States — must confront the problem of governance brought about by a multiplicity of values and opinions.

It is difficult for Americans to concede that change is not always desirable. We are impatient people who believe that we can usually make our future better than the present. "The difficult we do right away; the impossible takes a bit longer." But whether the change leads to an orthodoxy of giantism or of diminution is irrelevant. Perhaps what this nation must learn is Lord Falkland's dictum, "When it is not necessary to change, it is necessary not to change."

The myth that small is beautiful looks attractive during present period when the size of government is equated with inefficiency. Unfortunately, the experience with decentralized institutions does not augur well, either, for efficient governing units. What we require is a strong and vigorous government, one that can establish direction and realize its aims. It is not Gullivers that we need, nor is it Lilliputians. It is simply effective institutions, clear and attainable goals, and competent people.

Chapter 7

Myth of Work

"Work keeps at bay three great evils: boredom, vice, and need."

Voltaire

"All work, even cotton-spinning, is noble; work is alone noble."

Thomas Carlyle

"Work expands so as to fill the time available for its completion (and) the thing to be done swells in importance and complexity in a direct ratio with the time to be spent."

C. Northcote Parkinson

Saint Paul's dictum, "If a man will not work, neither shall he eat" is as much a part of the American ethos as baseball, Big Macs and Coca Cola. But over the last two decades Saint Paul's basic law of nature has been so revised that it might now read "If a man will not work, we will nevertheless make sure he eats." The idea together with the actual condition of work has changed dramatically. Curiously, however, neither the recipients of government largesse nor those who pay the taxes are content with the existing arrangement. In fact, it can be argued that arguments that were once employed to buttress the myth have been emasculated.

The Protestant Ethic, for example, is now reserved exclusively for lower socioeconomic levels, what Peter Berger has described as "the *blueing* of America." But even if the virtues of diligence, punctuality, honesty, and rectitude are translated into worldly success, they are cynically derided by the "new class" as expressions of servitude. In those occupying the seats of power, one can observe very few models of bourgeois virtue.

Another former rationalization for work was Social Darwinism. This theory explaining success as a function of survival of the fittest reduces social exchange to the laws of nature. But work and its attendant rewards are not easily explained — and certainly not easily accepted — when they are shrouded in a biological process over which men seemingly have no control.

Perhaps the most powerful contemporary argument for a work mythology that has been vitiated in the last ten years is the belief that technology has introduced entirely new standards of efficiency. "Work performance" has become a widely-used expression to measure this efficiency, yet the expression does not reflect its claim to legitimacy. Efficiency and success are tenuously related. Very often the conditions that lead to success are unpredictable. Therefore, doing good may not lead to good, a condition that has undermined the infatuation with efficiency as the bellwether of work.

For centuries, one's identity, psychological well-being and economic security were associated with the job. It is no coincidence that so many Americans are named Smith, Carpenter, Cooper, Chandler, Farmer, Baker, or Miller. Work was once an intrinsic condition of life. As the linkage between work and identity became attenuated, "the search for identity" became a national pastime. In *La Dolce Vita,* Marcello Mastroianni characterizes modern man, or the man of the cybernetic age, when, with elegant clothes on his back and even more elegant women dangling from each arm, he longingly glances at a workman with shovel in hand, sweat glistening on his back. For modern man, the privileges of success are not translated into the "meaningful" life. One would expect the workman to envy him; instead, the reverse occurs. This is not simply a trick from Fellini's well-developed imagination; it is the belief that life without work is vacuous.

As unlikely a collection of people as Calvin, Marx, and Freud made the same point, although each relied on a distinctive view of work to enjoin their respective ideological visions. For Calvin work (read: "good work") was the consequence of predestination, a tangible sign of one's salvation. "Good works don't [necessarily] make a good man, but a good man makes good work." What is necessary in Calvin's view is the freedom to demonstrate one's goodness. An ethic of individual responsibility provided the psychological attitude, personal discipline, and rationale for a faith in advancement through work. Poverty, when it existed, was not ignored, but it was considered a providential decree of a person's weakness. Its cure, therefore, was a heightened sense of personal responsibility; and when that was not possible, as in the case of the infirm, individuals would be *assigned* to care for those unable to care for themselves.

On his part, Marx was principally concerned with the exploitation of workers in a capitalist economy. But he also anticipated a time when automation would replace most of the workers, thereby creating a mass of disaffected potential revolutionaries. While this condition did not occur and is not likely to occur in a social-welfare environment, it does suggest that Marx recognized work labor as a stabilizing social force. Presumably, to him the only *bête noire* of capitalism is unemployment.

Finally, Freud envisioned work as the sublimation of libidinal drives. According to his analysis, some degree of personal expression must be sacrificed in order to meet the demands of civilization. The price an individual pays for living in a stable society may be neurosis, a neurosis characterized by restrained libidinal expression and sublimated libidinal energy. But the trade-off in bourgeois culture is social stability, personal rewards through work and the maintenance of law in return for some limitation on individual freedom. Labor becomes a key ingredient in the calculus. It allows for some expression in an environment where control is a necessity and it provides the rewards that are the incentive for loyalty to the social system.

While there is general agreement that work is necessary for the maintenance of a stable social order and for individual fulfillment, there are forces set loose by prosperity and exaggerated expectations that call into question the myth of work. One of these is the disestablishment of religion, a development which has placed inordinate demands on the social system. Demands made in the name of "fulfillment" have become strident and unreasonable. What in the past might have been a consolation for frustration, e.g. an afterlife, or the acceptance of a social contract in order to obtain stability, no longer applies. A stoical resignation to one's work as a duty has given way to the false myth of work as fulfilling and providing both extrinsic material and psychic rewards. Without a sense of obligation, work has become a mere means to an end. Thus, many people take jobs only because it affords them the resources, and a long weekend, to go skiing. Work itself is viewed peripherally.

It is clear that the dynamics of self-realization have undermined the bourgeois work ethic. In subverting this tradition, the spokesmen for self-realization have damaged the very system that supports personal fulfillment! By emphasizing the uncompromisingly personal, the liberationists have lost sight of one's public responsibility; even their work is defined as an essentially private act. But can a society exist with work that is so atomized?

Since the end of World War II, the West has transformed its economic systems to incorporate: the manifest desire for the welfare state, the need for a new, huge managerial and professional class, and the bohemian standards of popular culture as middle-class hedonism. Each of these factors has, in turn, vitiated the useful myth of work.

Economically, the need for government spending led to increased taxes and an inability to modernize the industrial plant. While there is some variation in this claim from industry to industry, steel production stands out as one egregious example of the general problem. As a result of this inability to modernize, some economies stagnate. Growth in production is not possible when capital cannot be invested. The conclusion is invariably static industry and few new jobs.

Compounding this problem is the growing anti-business bias of the new class, a class which is oriented to public-sector politics. The focus of new-class politics is a leftist-leaning political posture that opposes the growth of industry. Its class interests — to the extent they can be defined — are in the protection of management and professional areas, not industrial positions. Their jobs are ostensibly cerebral while their work is cut off from the elemental aspects of work activity, which is the foundation of most employment.

Another factor affecting attitudes towards work is found in the fact that the moral relativism resulting from post-war events has now expanded to encompass middle-class attitudes. A feeling of letting-go has contaminated the underpinnings of capitalism that rely on sobriety, loyalty, punctuality, and industry.

But perhaps the factor that has been most damaging to the work ethos is the emerging redefinition of equality. As already noted, equality-of-opportunity has been challenged by equality-of-result. The belief that discrimination based on a particular group attribute is unjust has been challenged by the demand that one must have a place primarily because he possesses a group attribute, or belongingness. The individual person is not judged; only his group affiliation matters. This philosophy has dramatically affected merit, however inexact that is, as a criterion for job selection. If one's good will is determined by a head count of those having a certain group affiliation, hard and good work are of relatively little value in the social equation. As a result, spiritual malaise concerning work is inevitable. Rightly or wrongly, no one wants to pay the price for historical malfeasance. Moreover, fairness warrants an opportunity for all.

Implicit in the decisions to press for equality-of-result is the catalyst for disruption, conflict, and cynicism about work. Workers, not having the desired attribute, are disfavored as their counterparts with the desired attribute once were. This principle runs counter to the entire liberal tradition of our history. If some persons were to be better off, it was maintained, the less advantaged were also to be better off. If one gained, so must others. The presumption was that social order is dependent on a fair distribution of opportunity. Surely, this didn't always occur. But the preeminence of the goal and myth remained unaltered. We now have a fundamental shift in values in which a view of merit "from each according to his ability, to each according to his ability" has been changed to the Marxist shibboleth of "from each according to his ability, to each according to his need."

The incentive to work, as understood by capitalist prescriptions, has been lost. It is, I might add, not simply the pursuit of material rewards that has caused this loss. The issue revolves about the notion of fairness. Few would deride the priority of the disadvantaged in social policy, but not at the risk of diminishing opportunity for others to rise to the top through work and effort. Yet, this is what appears to be going on. I say "appears," since the appearance is as important as the reality. A decline in incentive may be due as much to perceptions as to actual conditions. Even minimal efforts to impute numerical standards to group attributes has the effect of magnifying antagonisms and bringing to the surface charges of injustice.

In an effort to eliminate social inequality, the government has employed access to education as a means to obtain status through credentials and income through jobs requiring high-level skills. In so doing, it has nurtured attitudes of "entitlement" to good jobs among those with college degrees. But the economic system appears incapable, during this period of stagnant economic growth, of keeping pace with the inflation of employment expectations. Simply put, there are not enough high-level jobs for all those people who want them or who believe that they qualify for them. Paradoxically, the well-intended social and educational policies of the government are engendering frustration among the very college-educated students financed by government programs.

The response has been a general skepticism toward work and a reexamination of the university's purpose. In the former case, college graduates, believing themselves over-qualified for manual jobs and incapable of meeting the requirements for the few high level jobs available, have become a potential powder keg of discontent. In the latter case, a university organized to promote and sustain the ideals of a free society has become preoccupied with job training and vocationalism, losing sight of its traditional mission.

What has been undermined in this era of ideological conflict and social change is the myth that work has its own, intrinsic rewards. With this change in consciousness, a mythical construct that served to stabilize the society has been undermined. The myth once provided the character of shared experience; it underwrote meaning to the culture. A loss of such meaning only prompts incomprehensions which cannot be tolerated; the void inevitably produces a search for new meaning. Since much of the character of people and their social arrangements is determined by their work, the removal of the work ethos generates the fear that the next chapter in this nation's historical tale will be disruptive or, even worse, simply vacuous.

Obviously, the litmus test of this mythical debunking cannot be found in the gross reduction of the work week. In its simplest form, the evaluation is predicated on the amount of time given to the production of social goods in relation to the time given to the consumption of private enjoyment. Since the latter has now overtaken, also dictates to the former, there is no question but that work has lost its meaning. A composite picture of a Veblenesque world has engulfed us, a world in which opulence is defined by personal consumption and private time away from the job. It is the poor who must live for economic realities. The affluent have less interest in greater wealth — hence less interest in work — and more of a concern than was ever the case in immediate gratification.

A formidable task for the future of our society will be the effort to make work a creative and desirable activity. We will once again have to ask what are the appropriate moral and market incentives for work and secondarily what are the appropriate welfare benefits for those who do not toil. We will be obliged to consider what is the necessity for further public sector growth and how can the private sector be stimulated. We must recognize — perhaps we already do — that in this period of finite resources economic growth will be limited, but hard and productive work is essential. How, then, do we move from this Disneylike phantasmagoria of play to meet the challenges demanded by economic realities:

It is not far-fetched to reconsider the traditional myth of work. Joseph Conrad argued that transforming the unknown into clear forms is the *raison d'etre* for civilization. "To be safe, civilized man must have a blind devotion to immediate practical tasks, a devotion which recalls the Victorian cult of work," suggests J. Hillis Miller. Work is unquestionably a protection against personal doubt, an antidote to the paralysis of will. We sometimes forget that work is a shield against the thin crust of civility — to use John Maynard Keynes' phrase — that can turn into ferocious destruction. We need our work on a personal and symbolic level as the society needs work to retain its vitality. Perhaps the need will lead us to the myth before the disappearance of the myth leads us to the abyss.

Chapter 8

Myth of Poverty

"I can get no remedy against this consumption of the purse: borrowing only lingers and lingers it out, but the disease is incurable."

William Shakespeare

"Who does not know that much of our so called philanthropy tends to blunt the edge of our moral perception and, consequently, to perpetuate those conditions which seem to make philanthropy necessary?"

Henry Adams

There are issues on which there is extraordinary consensus in our society. Poverty, I submit, is one such matter. People may disagree on the policy that should be employed to eradicate the problem, but almost no one will describe poverty as desirable. That, ironically, may explain why one of the most persistent and pernicious cultural myths has evolved over this issue. Stated very directly, it is the belief that the government has a responsibility to set a floor on poverty, to do what is necessary to bring each individual up to or over that level. It should be kept in mind that the present "poverty level" is not based on any measure of absolute poverty; rather it is a standard of relative deprivation institutionalized and made concrete by social-science research.

Needless to say, policies of any kind are usually based on prevailing attitudes. Nutritional needs, for example, are related to the demands of occupation and leisure time. They may also be a function of expectations: Although steer liver is more nutritionally desirable and less expensive than filet mignon, the filet is usually preferred. A comprehensive nutritional policy based on eating preferences would inferentially suggest that the poor have an equal opportunity for arteriosclerosis. Health needs are influenced by longevity; education needs by personal goals; and self-actualization by surplus income.

Poverty and policies affecting poverty are inextricably woven into the fabric of historical development. It is obviously inappropriate to discuss the poverty of one locale without relating it to the social evolution of a nation. In examining attitudes toward poverty, therefore, one must actually examine the social context in which poverty exists. Even then, what must be considered are those cataclysmic events such as war, prosperity, and inflation that give poverty definition and those legislative policies that create a "poverty level" for political purposes.

By mid-century, it could be maintained that a conventional wisdom based on government assistance had been established. This attitude of mind included the following characteristics:

1. Aid to the dependent poor is their right, not a privilege;
2. Dependency not only involves the absence of "sufficient funds" but "psychological deprivation," a deprivation often cited as a key factor in the recurring condition of family poverty;
3. The society should assume responsibility for poverty, not the poor themselves;
4. Legal service should be provided for all the poor in order to prevent state elimination of their right to assistance;
5. Aid does not suppose only welfare or subsistence but also sufficient funds and services to provide a "decent" standard of living.

What these assumptions suggest is that sometime between the New Deal period and the mid 1960's, the reluctant but irreversible direction of further federal government involvement in poverty matters became an active and affirmative commitment to eliminate the presence of poverty. The Progressive spirit manifested as moral concern became a political program.

With the violence and national soul-searching that characterized the urban riots of the sixties came a challenge to the classic liberal assumption that continuous expansion of the Gross National Product at the 4 or 5 percent annual rate would ultimately lead to the elimination of poverty. It was obvious that the expansion of the GNP did not affect entrenched pockets of poverty that were resistant to the general expansion of national wealth. Liberals were forced to choose — this is what polarization was all about — between a respect for law that overlooked the conditions of poverty and a demonstration of immediate concern for the poor that overlooked law, precedents, and previous policy. The decision to opt for a War on Poverty revealed which direction the Democratic-dominated government took.

Whether one accepts the argument that poverty policies were directly related to political realignments in the inner-city or the view that administrative neglect and ignorance of the consequences created an atmosphere whereby temporary, makeshift programs became permanent, the fact remains that politics in the decade of the sixties dictated a set of poverty reforms. These reforms were reinforced by institutions organized to eliminate "the poverty problem." For example, legal services successfully challenged state efforts to limit welfare eligibility; government agencies organized the poor to picket welfare departments as part of a legitimate strategy for further assistance; the Office of Economic Opportunity contended that participation of the poor in policy making was necessary to overcome the psychological deprivation of powerlessness; and welfare rights groups were organized to demand increased assistance to dependent people. In most respects, the tentative character of early twentieth-century reforms became entrenched policies and the arguments for government assistance dictated practice.

The sensitizing of a generally affluent population to the conditions of poverty — through such works as Michael Harrington's *Other America* — a climate of concern created in which entitlements were made possible. It became commonplace in the late sixties and early seventies to observe welfare recipients who owned color television sets organize and picket for a guaranteed income. They were joined in the "struggle" for entitlements by guilt-ridden liberals, unreconstructed New Dealers, and idealists of various persuasions who sought an identification with the downtrodden for what Edward Banfield described as a need for "psychic satisfaction." There were, of course, the needy desperate for assistance and the social reformers with genuine motives for their involvement. But with the overheated rhetoric of the period, it was difficult to make distinctions.

In short order, *wants* replaced *needs*; to use Aristotelian terms, "wants by their nature are unlimited and unsatiable." Since attitudes toward consumption had been freed from the constraints of the Protestant Ethic in the affluent post-war era, and since many of the affluent believed there was enough to go around for everyone, accumulation of goods and a right to possess them became inalienable. Even with a major recession upon us, the expectation of rising benefits and entitlements remains undiminished.

Where poverty of the nineteenth century was viewed as inevitable, a part of the ebb and flow of history, it is now considered an aberration of the times that can be eliminated merely by governmental formula. This attitude is perpetuated as a vested interest by administrations that reject the notion only on pain of risking their political survival.

What emerges from this brief survey of attitudes toward poverty and welfare proposals is the appearance of a myth. For much of American history, poverty was regarded as either a natural condition influenced by providence or a function of character flaws. In either event, social assistance, while always existing, was strictly limited to those cases where no other means of support was available. What society demanded was contrition from the poor, a well-developed sense of self-help from the general population. The strain in this belief came with extended depressions in which some actual employables, eager to work, could not find jobs. As a consequence, personal responsibility gave way to social responsibility. Aid evolved from a privilege to a practice, thence to a right and an entitlement. George Homans perspicaciously explained this process when he noted: "Precedents are always turning into rights."

The change in attitude toward poverty resulted in both a quantitative as well as qualitative change in what it meant to be poor. During the sixties — a period of relative affluence despite spiraling inflation — the welfare rolls escalated dramatically in every major city. Conditions could not be described as worse than the previous decade, but our perception of them had changed. Poverty was simply not acceptable, not for the most affluent nation in the world, a nation that had, moreover, marshalled its resources for a war against it.

Just as public assistance moved from a privilege to a right, poverty itself changed from a condition of unfortunate circumstances that required temporary relief to a situation that warranted affection, friendship, psychological treatment, and massive public concern. Social work meant more than processing names on relief rolls; it was a public service that required an analysis of the symptoms of "social pathology," which led to the conclusion, more often than not, that the poor are the flotsam and jetsam of industrialization, "pawns of capitalism."

That the attendant problems of poverty — like crime and apathy — remained even when the poor had more money was one of those social facts that was conspicuously ignored by those with a vested interest in the maintenance of assistance programs. The irresistible force of a bureaucracy with a stake in assisting the poor perpetuates the idea of "poverty levels." Meantime, a well-developed sense of social responsibility on the part of many of the affluent and government officials eager to maintain political support with poor constitutuents only contributes to the notion that poverty can be eliminated by government fiat.

Meanwhile, conditions do improve — even if there is disagreement on how much. But as the relative difference in income declines, especially between the working-poor and welfare-poor, the class differences that remain are exaggerated. To illustrate: Between 1936 and 1950 the income of the highest quintile of all income recipients rose by 32 percent, and the income of the lowest quintile by 125 percent. Furthermore, from 1956 to 1967 median white income rose 46.6 percent while median black income rose 76.2 percent. "By 1970 there remained no difference between young (under 35) husband-and-wife families, white or black." Yet, the trend toward equalization that pervaded the entire structure did not create widespread satisfaction. It is axiomatic that there is little competition for status between the person who earns $10,000 and the one who earns $50,000 a year; while there is likely to be more envy when one earns $10,000 and another earns $12,000 for similar work.

It may very well be that the egalitarian surge of the past two decades cannot be resisted. Some form of guaranteed income establishing greater equality than the present tax system is likely — which accounts in no small part for the growing popularity of the negative income tax. But the paradox in providing further aid to the poor is that more aid creates more "poverty." Attitudes toward poverty have conspired to create a situation where the more aid we have the worse it gets. With more aid and more social workers than ever before, and a heightened sense of social responsibility, the welfare rolls grow and the poor are increasingly disenchanted.

If a female-headed family of three in New York City obtained an income — including welfare payments, medical assistance, clothing allowance, rent subsidies, food stamps — of $11,500 in 1973 and the average family income in the city in that year was $10,500, a disincentive to work and an incentive to go on welfare clearly existed. Empirically, entitlements work where everyone enjoys equal benefits for relatively equal output. But that is not the prevailing attitude. Wants appear to have outstripped *gives* by a substantial margin. And if anything is true, it is that more people want more for less than was ever the case. Even if the unlikely egalitarian utopia suggested by John Rawls were upon us, equality could exist only when expectations are curbed, when people will produce more and accept less.

Our present attitudes have already become an indulgence we can ill afford. In New York City, for example, from 1960 to 1973 the number of persons on welfare tripled while the rate of unemployment was halved. But, as one would guess, in the same period there was a notorious shortage of unskilled labor. Jobs remained unfilled because the price of poverty was higher than, or comparable to, the price of labor. As long as the system suggests that it pays to be poor, the government can expect the poverty level to rise to the price being offered. Moreover, as long as the government depends for its support on various forms of public assistance, the national debt will increase, and those living at the margin or on a fixed income, will be driven to despair. In the long run, it does not require a sophisticated imagination to conceive of a scenario of rebellion and conflict over the issue of who works and who doesn't, and who pays the taxes for those who receive the assistance. In consideration of conditions like these, Pitirim Sorokin noted, societies rise and fall on their attitude toward poverty, equality, and privilege.

Chapter 9

Myth of Psychology

"Therapists become the principal allies in the struggle for composure; we turn to them in the hope of achieving the modern equivalent of salvation, 'mental health'."

Christopher Lasch

"There is in psychology today a general background assumption that the human impulses provided by biological evolution are right and optimal, both individually and socially, and that repressive or inhibitory moral traditions are wrong. Psychology, in propagating this background perspective in its teaching of perhaps 80 or 90 percent of college undergraduates, and increasing proportions of high school pupils, helps to undermine the retention of what may be extremely valuable social-evolutionary inhibitory systems which we do not yet fully understand."

Donald Campbell
former president of the
American Psychological
Association

Each day there are Americans who engage in primal screams, acts of self-abuse, groping, meditation, jumping, imposed constipation, reenactments of birth and free-associating — all in an effort to discover "mental health." These millions of people are explorers searching the uncharted terrain of the mind in a vain attempt to find an understanding of the self and then, presumably, "peace of mind." This frenetic activity occurs with the often unknowing or reluctant imprimatur of the discipline of psychology, a field of examination responsible for the myth that "secular salvation" is available through the application of psychological techniques.

Result: a myth has emerged that is based on the facile assumption that mankind can achieve psychic repose if it can be liberated from the "bourgeois ethos." Christopher Lasch writes: "To liberate humanity from such outmoded ideas of love and duty has become the mission of the post-Freudian therapies and particularly of their converts and popularizers, for whom mental health means the overthrow of inhibitions and immediate gratification of every impulse."

According to Dr. Leonard Crammer, a New York psychiatrist and author of *Freedom From Compulsion*, there are many people who are uptight, neurotic about moral inhibitions and overly concerned about fulfilling obligations conscientiously. The cure is simple: relax. Live with problems and "simply assume that if the worst happens, I'll pay the price, along with everyone else."

To test ourselves and make sure we are not one of the uptight types, Crammer has devised an obsessive-compulsive personality inventory that permits self-rating. Several of the values on this scale reveal a great deal about what Dr. Crammer considers appropriate behavior at this time: "I get upset if I don't finish a task;" "I like everything I do to be perfect;" "I do things precisely to the last detail;" "I plan my time so that I won't be late;" "It bothers me when my surroundings are not clean and tidy;" "I think that I expect worthy moral standards in others;" "I think that I am sexually inhibited;" "I find myself working rather than relaxing;" "I like to budget myself carefully and live on a cash and carry basis."

According to the scoring, if we adhere to these values none or a little or some of the time, it is better than adhering to them a good part or most of the time. If one extrapolates from this scoring system and makes assumptions about the values therein, it appears as if noncompletion is better than completion of a task; imperfection is better than perfection; lateness is better than promptness; sloppiness is better than tidiness; avoiding obligations is better than fulfilling them; expecting moral standards in others is worse than not expecting them; promiscuity is better than sexual inhibition; relaxation is better than work; being social is better than being private; and being profligate is better than being thrifty.

Of course, Dr. Crammer would disagree with this contention. If one is "uptight, insecure and driving hard," the answer is "to ease off," which translates into relaxation of the values.

From my point of view, this attitude reflects another of the many assaults on traditional bourgeois values launched by the community of psychologists. By assuming that we should live with problems, i.e., "adjust" to them, the implicit concern and probable effect is complacency. Don't worry about doing a better job; relax and enjoy yourself. Presumably, enjoyment should be encouraged at the risk of jeopardizing hard work, effort, obligations, and morality. In the process, the beneficiary will become less neurotic. What is ignored by Dr. Crammer, and by far too many of his colleagues, is the effect this relaxed attitude has on society.

"Feel good about yourself," "don't worry so much about commitments," are the admonitions to a society that has been described as abnormal for believing — or is it *having* believed? — in delayed gratification, the imperfection of human beings and the observance of commitments. The new order encourages us to act for any purpose whatever, so long as we don't feel uptight but do feel relaxed.

In the extreme, one can envision a social system that promotes anarchic behavior with the only concern being over the "feeling of self-worth," regardless of the acts committed. "It isn't bad that I don't work, it's bad that I can't relax and enjoy the free time." "It isn't the crime that's bad, but whether I feel guilty about it." Standards in this scenario are based on whim. This is psychological existentialism gone wild.

All that I can hope for is that when crime is even more prevalent than at present, when the garbage isn't collected, when the arrival of mail is based on feelings, that bourgeois guilt may be reintroduced as nourishment for the survival of civilization, even if we become a little neurotic in the process.

Interestingly, a recent lead story in *Time* magazine, entitled "Psychiatry on the Couch," made the point that even the professionals are skeptical of what the discipline can accomplish. Well-publicized anti-psychiatry psychiatrists like Thomas Szasz argue that there is no such thing as mental illness at all, only a variety of responses to the problems of living. While R. D. Laing has made the observation that psychosis may indeed be "far superior to normal experience."

Psychotherapy is a treatment designed to discover the sources of an emotional problem in order to effectuate an attitudinal change. The therapist usually listens, and interprets. His assumption is that the problem is related to deep-seated and learned motives and beliefs. Presumably, when the patient is aware of motives, he will solve the concealed problem.

But how does the psychotherapist determine which motive, attitude and belief causes the emotional distress? Since there are so many schools of thought, contradiction and confusion abound. A Freudian, Jungian, Adlerian, Reichian, Rogerian would each diagnose the problem in a different way and prescribe different treatment. Can it be argued that any therapist, regardless of his position, is equally qualified to help a patient? Furthermore, it should also be asked whether abnormal behavior is a response to "learned attitudes" concealed in the psyche and can thus be unlearned or whether some forms of abnormality have nothing at all to do with "learned attitudes." Moreover, what precisely do mysterious and intriguing concepts such as "penis envy," "superego," "Oedipus complex," "Electra complex," "collective unconscious" mean? Do they obfuscate more than they reveal? Do they so rivet our minds as interesting ideas that we are distracted from what is concrete, real and perhaps the source of emotional woe?

If these phrases were simply interesting ideas that entertained and titillated, that would be one thing; but they masquerade as secular ethics. Thomas Szasz has referred to psychotherapy as "the religion of the formally irreligious." Explicitly, it has substituted for religion a normative perception of life that avoids the Judeo Christian heritage and relies on a jargon laden positivist treatment of maladjustment. In fact, the rhetoric is equated with remedy. Take this exchange between therapist and patient as an illustration:

> Psychotherapist: How do you feel about your mother?
>
> Patient: I don't know. I guess there are times when I'm annoyed with her, yet I know I care.
>
> Psychotherapist: Tell me about the times you're annoyed. What annoys you most?
>
> Patient: Her complaints, her telling me what to do.
>
> Psychotherapist: Was it always this way?

Patient: As long as I can remember.
Psychotherapist: Aren't there times you hate her?
Patient: Hate? I wouldn't say that.
Psychotherapist: But if you did say that, wouldn't
                 you feel better?

In this case the patient can't win. Unless he express-
es a hate he may not actually feel, he cannot feel better. The
proof is in the pudding, even though the pudding may not exist.

The essence of psychotherapy is an immediate response to a perceived problem based on consensual standards of
adjustment. There is an inclination to dismiss all "nonscientific"
problems, particularly questions about man's nature. Since issues
of this kind are not subject to inquiry, assumed scientific approaches of psychotherapy suggest that they are not worth discussing at all. There is no human nature for psychotherapists,
only human behavior. They either do not make value judgments
or they discount them. "Good" and "bad" are terms reserved
for the religious zealots and have no place in the psychotherapists
lexicon. Within the expanding borders of permissive culture, considerations of sin and guilt, as well as of individual responsibility,
have become antiquated. There are many urbane people who,
like Aldous Huxley's seedy decadents, would prefer to be caught
in the act of adultery rather than face a charge of provincialism.

Psychotherapists reject the idea that it is their duty
to so change social forces that man's goodness may be resur-
rected. They respond to what is, not what might be. Their views
are determined by the faith in their jargon. People are simply
here; what they will do, they will do. There is no universal purpose. There are no absolutes. And if God is in his heaven, he has
no effect on our behavior.

What emerges from this psychotherapeutic analysis
is a relativity of relativism. Only what you believe to be true or,
stated differently, only what applies to you is significant. But
after undergoing therapy, after imbibing the non-religious and
essentially egoist message, after searching for *the* cause of your
psychic problem, does it make any difference? Like Somerset
Maugham who travels all the way to a New-found-land, the
psychotherapist's patient travels the road of therapy to find only
himself. If there is no responsibility, if there is no higher belief,
except the prevailing standard of the moment, then man is free to
embrace the excesses of his own self-appreciation. Through
psychology, man can avoid the value judgments of tradition and
provide himself with all the latitude and license his desire may
seek.

Chapter 10

The Myth of Experimental Art

"If the artificial is not better than the natural, to what end are all the arts of life?"

John Stuart Mill

At a recent lecture on contemporary art at New York University, the lecturer was asked, "How do you know whether the work is good?" Somewhat taken aback, the lecturer responded, "if the work is creative." Still perplexed, the student countered, "But how do you determine what's creative?" With much less hesitation this time, the lecturer said, "In modern art creativity can be equated with novelty."

Those words were indelibly etched in my brain: "Creativity equals novelty." The meaning is bizarre, albeit revealing. In order to be creative, presumably one must do something different. Here is the latest social justification for doing your own thing. Whether the artist demonstrates skill, discipline and knowledge is unimportant. What counts is whether his work is *different*. With this kind of interpretation the normative dimensions of the good and beautiful are reduced to personal whim.

61

What happened to standards? Where are those consensual values that determine artistic taste? And how does one decide what is good and bad? In a world of impermanence and novelty, artistic standards that had legitimacy for the design of a cultural conception are gone. As Henry James noted, cultural standards are hard to obtain and, by implication, harder to maintain: ". . . it takes an endless amount of history to make even a little tradition, and an endless amount of tradition to make even a little taste . . ."

And taste is apparently what we lack. Perhaps this example will illustrate the point. Recently, I was invited to an artistic happening by a well-known art critic. With some anticipation — based on his praise — I looked forward to this "major event."

Inside a darkened theatre appeared a woman on the stage who did a rather tasteful striptease. She revealed a well-preserved body that was artfully contoured. With her birthday suit as her canvas, she proceeded to jump in a giant vat of chocolate pudding. She rubbed the pudding all over her body with special attention to her orifices and then left the stage. There was no applause, nor were there any Brooklyn boos, although I must admit to a powerful temptation to offer one.

Startled by what had gone on, I asked my host to explain. "Why she's one of the most talented 'body artists' in the world," he said. "Body artist, what does that mean?" I asked, with more than a little annoyance. He replied that she had used her body for artistic expression. "Suppose" — I contended — "that I disrobe and jump into the chocolate pudding. Would that too be artistic expression?" "Well, maybe, but keep in mind that you weren't the first to do it."

It isn't possible to generalize from this experience of course. But once again the element of novelty was equated with creativity. I wonder whether being the first to wear a body suit of star spangled ribbons would make me an artist or perhaps sleeping on a bed covered with jello. It was interesting to note that no one at the happening was willing to say that the " emperor had no clothes." Since she did indeed have no clothes, which anyone could admit, the analogue isn't appropriate. But anyone could also tell that she didn't demonstrate any artistic talent; yet, on this point there were no admissions either.

This sobering experience caused me to worry about my friend. Why does a noted art critic accept this nonsense? Does he have heightened artistic sensibilities that I don't understand? Does he apply a standard of judgement based on years of experience? Or am I simply a hopeless philistine? Rather than ask insensitive questions, I decided to read his criticism. It was very revealing. After reading at least three dozen reviews, I didn't find one that could be interpreted as critical. Even when he seemed to rouse himself to find fault with an artist's work, he either apologized for the remark or balanced it with praise. Although she was writing about book reviewing, my friend's criticism reminded me of a comment Elizabeth Hardwick offered two decades ago:

"Sweet, bland commendations fall everywhere upon the scene. A universal, if somewhat lobotomized, accommodation reigns. A book is born into a puddle of treacle; the brine of hostile criticism is only a memory. Everyone is found to have 'filled a need,' and is to be 'thanked' for something and to be excused for 'minor faults in an otherwise excellent work'."

That this should be the state of reviewing suggests a great deal about standards, something about back-scratching and, I suspect, a little about investments. What critic, except perhaps the ever acerbic John Simon, is willing to become a target for the very people he attacks? Which one is willing to risk exclusion from major art events? How many critics, with the influence to make careers, resist the obvious temptation to buy a work at rock bottom prices before the review skyrockets them to six figures? How dispassionate will a critic be about a work of art when it opposes his political beliefs? Frances FitzGerald criticized the "Deerhunter" because the film didn't conform to her political interpretation of the Vietnam War while she commended "Coming Home" because it did. How critical of Warren Beatty's films was Pauline Kael when she was in his employ?

To a great extent the lack of critical standards is due to a cultural vacuousness in the society. Since the artists don't know what the expectations are, they opt for the different and bizarre, all of which is excused by the experimental label. Critics are unwilling to criticize because the ground rules aren't clear. A student of mine, after attending a poetry reading, exclaimed: "I didn't have the foggiest idea of what he was talking about. It was so dense, it must have been important." She isn't a professional critic but her judgement is no more perplexing that the pros.

When one reads the work of critics, it becomes obvious that the widely-used judgmental terms only express the widely-held ambiguity about contemporary art. Long ago, I discovered that "cool," as opposed to warm and not chic, is a popular expression that, when it is applied to a painting, becomes utterly baffling. Does it describe purpose or effect? Another favorite word is "expressive," a term that can be attributed to just about anything from dancing to salivating. Still another widely used expression is "free-form." Free-form is also contrasted with rigidity, although it seems to me it should be contrasted with discipline. Whenever an artistic presentation lacks form, rhythm, and comprehension it is free-form. And the last chestnut is exploratory: This term is employed for artists who are engaged in a self-described "odyssey" to find their "natural mode of expression." I'm not sure this mode is ever discovered. But while the search is on, the work of these artists is, well, exploratory!

One example of how density may be made to equal profundity was amply illustrated by the generally warm reception given by American critics to Jean Luc Godard's films. After Godard's first and best film, "Breathless," he subsequently made films that were consistent with his orthodox Marxist predilections. There is nothing wrong with that except that he insisted on testing the patience of his audiences with two-hour monologues by stoop-shouldered revolutionaries who read Leninist tracts with about as much enthusiasm as fifth graders do when they read the multiplication tables. No matter how one rationalized them — and there were many attempts — Godard's films were disliked even by the Marxists, albeit they would never admit that to non-Marxists. Yet, even when the rare reviewer would criticize Godard — usually for his incredibly slow pacing — nevertheless there was a positive gesture made for his "courageous experimentalism." Why a talking head reading from *Das Capital* should be a courageous artistic experiment I'll never know! Since the camera focuses on a garrulous figure, I suspect that anyone who can handle a Brownie can make one of Godard's films. This may seem grossly unfair. But is it any more unfair than having to sit through his films?

Perhaps the prince of the boring although "experimental" art world is Andy Warhol. His film, entitled "Sleep," showing a man sleeping for eight hours, was probably a statement on the attention Warhol deserves. His art is quite literally the trash of an abundant society, e.g., Ajax containers, Campbell's soup cans. Surely, we are often incapable of recognizing the aesthetic quality in many of our products. But when it is brought to our attention, shouldn't we give credit to the original commercial artist, not the trash collector who puts the object in a frame? Why, then, is Warhol ensconced in a place of honor in the art world? The answer which appears time and again in print is his experimentalism. Because he did what no one else did, his work is legitimized by the shared belief in artistic iconoclasm. It also helps to have the right friends, a lesson in which Mr. Warhol has earned an unofficial Ph.D.

I firmly believe that art is a barometer of social attitudes. It isn't neutral; it both debases and edifies by example. But if art is nothing but impulse, everyone is an artist. And if one accepts this democratic supposition, then no one is an artist. Like characters out of Moliere's *The Misanthrope*, art critics heap so much praise on so many for so little that the praise and criticism are indistinguishable.

Art-as-experiment is a pernicious myth because it obscures a necessary sense of discrimination. It becomes difficult in a culture where anything goes to determine what is beautiful, what is lovely. The debates about pornography and art prove this point. In a culture that is unsure of what is artistic, an ordinance against prurience is meaningless. Unless we can distinguish between what is and isn't art, there is no standard at all.

During a recent presentation of "Wake Up, It's Time To Go To Bed," a member of the audience shouted, "This stinks, this play stinks." I happened to agree with this fellow but I wasn't sure whether he was a member of the cast. I sat there befuddled wondering if this might be part of the nonexistent dialogue. To make matters worse, one member of the audience after another left the theater passing comments about the actors as they departed. This, too, seemed contrived until I realized that only my wife and I constituted the audience. I wanted to justify my perseverance with some rationalization of artistic merit. But the fact was I couldn't tell if the audience response was rehearsed or not. I couldn't tell if this was some happening or put on or a genuine event. In fact, I wasn't even sure whether I was in the audience or part of the company. In short, I am a victim of the very confusion I cite. A myth of experimentation has obscured my vision of truth, a situation that may have universal application.

Chapter 11

Myth of Impotence

"Nothing is so weak and unstable as a reputation for power not based on force."

Tacitus

If recent history has accomplished anything, it is a redefinition of the future. Optimism — which characterized a view of the American future as late as fifteen years ago — has been replaced by fatalism. A general cultural formulation that hard work breeds success and will improve the future has retreated before the observation that hard work is for suckers and won't make a difference. Americans believed in optimism because — precisely because — their future was undetermined. People did things because they were convinced their efforts would shape tomorrow. And they did, because they believed they could.

Americans became habituated to something William James called "the belief in potency," a belief in man's ability to influence his destiny. Whether this belief was verifiable or warranted is unimportant; James realized that people should act in accordance with the belief in order to secure freedom, autonomy and "the noble life." In American history a belief in man's ability to shape the future was the national faith. It was what accounted for that peculiarly American blend of pragmatism and religion.

One need not be a social scientist to realize that this value is now moribund. Bourgeois culture, which perpetuated the idea of the indeterminate future, has been undermined by a competing belief system described by Lionel Trilling as "adversary culture." This is not only the adversary cult of Con III, Indian beads, gurus and L.S.D., but one that subscribes to the belief that individuals can do nothing to shape the future. The future is closed; it is as inexorable as a Marxist prognostication of assured capitalist doom.

One such view of an "inevitable future" is the twentieth century "science" of behaviorism. If the much abused B. F. Skinner can be cited as testimony, there exists the cast-iron effect of environment on human behavior. In his scenarios, science precludes a free choice of futures. Control will be achieved by the arrangement of the environment and by the demythologizing of notions such as freedom and dignity. Impotence enters the consciousness as "the good life." To speak of powerlessness today is chic — a little like Zen, EST or ouija boards, which are other manifestations of the same social malaise. From boardrooms to collective bedrooms, the refrain appears to be the same: "What can anyone do?"

An inability to do anything about anything has penetrated otherwise rational minds like a fever. At a time when some transcendent myth of action and unity is desperately needed, what has emerged is a national myth of impotence. This has happened so quickly and with such intensity that we quizzically observe the effect of this inertia, but have few explanations for its cause, and even fewer responses which can serve as remedy. We are hungry for a reinvigorating myth.

Although explanations of cause are always risky, there are conditions of contemporary life that masquerade as pernicious myths:

1. Technology dominates our very existence;

2. The Cold War has dissipated national will, which is now directed for dubious goals;

3. Most social and economic problems are subject to easy solution.

4. Cultural programming can adopt any values without offending the body-politic.

What is interesting about these explanations is that they have a momentum of their own. They are used as irrefutable claims from one end of the country to the other. Yet, they are dubious at best and probably specious.

Technology, the modern bogeyman, appears impersonal, but men and women do the programming and determine use. The effects of technology can be devastating to the environment, yet it also produces consumer goods on a scale unprecedented in history. If there are technological effects we don't like, they are subject to our influence. If the benefits are not equal to the cost, they will be eliminated or controlled. The price of technology rises to the level of social demand. When people are willing to sacrifice a result in order to have another perceived benefit, more often than not, that will occur. It is, of course, in the area of personal sacrifice that problems occur.

Writers, such as Jacques Ellul, have maintained that technology possesses an inexorable momentum of its own. It is his contention that once the commitment to and investment in 'le technique'' has been made, man is trapped, caught in the spiral of ever more technological advances. If the truncated computer generations suggest anything, it is the compelling nature of the Ellul position. However, the use of the technology is not predetermined. Even if one were to accept computerization as a fact of modern life, one does not have to accept the way in which it is deployed.

For example, the heralded unemployment that would ensue from automation has not occurred. In part this is related to an obvious market function that the advocates of impending doom did not anticipate. As manufacturing jobs disappeared the service industries became infinitely more important in the economy than they had been. The consequence of technology was not widespread unemployment, but dislocation to economic areas having the potential to expand. Certainly this transition caused difficulty for many; yet the result was not what many spokesmen would have us believe.

Similarly, the Cold War dissipated our energies, but it is hardly for dubious ends. Despite the inflated rhetoric of the last ten years and the view of revisionist historians, the United States has become a reluctant power, a nation obliged to fill power vacuums in order to maintain some semblance of international stability. It is misleading to discuss "the arrogance of power'' without reference to historical antecedents, particularly the American role in World War II. It is worse yet to discuss foreign policy as if it is beyond our control. Post-Vietnam foreign policy may be bleak, but that is mainly because we think of it that way. By signalling impotence, we have transferred initiative to our detractors. And the less initiative we have, the more powerlessness intrudes on decision-making. If we are unwilling to pay the price demanded by the Cold War, the most adroit diplomatic moves will not restore national potency.

American diplomacy in the post-Vietnam era is based on moralisms which conceal an unwillingness to use military force even when that is warranted. African policy, to the extent there is one, has become an exercise in contradictory ethics. Apartheid is verbally condemned, but ineffectual sanctions are imposed. Cuban troops on both sides of that continent are morally repellant to our president, but are a force for stability, says our former ambassador to the U.N.

With a populace that has lost its nerve to defend vital interests, with statesman that can't even define our interests, we have lost a sense of direction in foreign affairs. To conceal our spiritual weakness, a campaign in moral righteousness has been launched. But who is affected by our preaching? Do the Russians avoid African encroachments? Do Cuban troops return to their homeland? Is South Africa responsive to our demands? Do we as a nation feel better about ourselves? Couched in the rhetoric of this new era is an essential consideration of the modern world: The nation that will not act to defend its interests has few options in international affairs except platitudinous moralizing. This is the language and possibly the effect of impotence.

We have been so deluded by political promises that it is difficult to distinguish between what is possible and what we want. We are often told that poverty can be eliminated. But how can poverty be eliminated when it is a relative standard? Improved conditions, in other words, cannot eliminate a lower economic quartile, only pure equality can do that. If polluted streams are considered a problem, they can be made clean. But streams can be made clean only when personal sacrifices are made. If people consider clean streams more worthwhile than stable taxes or the use of energy sources, they will have them. If illiteracy is a problem, children should be taught to read. But why should students learn to read when we have become so obsessed with viewing television that an expanded definition of literacy has been accommodated by the schools? We are beseiged by a utopianism that is based on the false assumption of the social cure. When a cure is not available, the prescription is either redefinition of the problem or nihilistic action. In both instances the result is likely to be a feeling of hopelessness. As a result utopianism masquerades as good intentions but is in fact a corrosive influence in the body politic exacerbating impotence.

Yet, if the errors that account for impotence are so palpable, why isn't this contemporary mythology challenged? It is painfully obvious that many people have a stake in its retention. The technocrats, who monopolize decision-making because it is assumed they are endowed with special information, act to control the dissemination of data. The professional classes that reap great financial rewards will not jeopardize their status and influence by sharing their carefully guarded skills. Those who preach apocalypse, such as professional revolutionaries, have also profited by telling the government and foundation executives that only revolution will solve our woe. Paradoxically this state of inertia has a force of its own. At this time the myth of impotence has a vitality that stems from those who would use its debilitating influence for their own ends.

For a generation that has been educated by television programmers, impotence is the likely learned response. Television programming caters to a mythology of fantasy; there is no real and unreal, no genuine and false. There is only what is. In this era where so much of what we see is false, seeing is not believing. Our judgements are often confused by what we see. The past comes to us restored as the present and filtered through the values of pseudo-events. The Korean War becomes the setting for a situation comedy ("Mash"), the Cuban missile crisis a tele-drama and the President Kennedy's assassination a tele-trial. How then do we evaluate the issues on which our future depends?

Historical restoration takes the form of media kitsch, the future is behind us. What we will have are reruns of what we've already seen. It is predictable because contemporary culture follows technique. The dated and incredible theme of interplanetary strife has been restyled in the fashion of modern technique and for the foreseeable future, will dictate the development of one phase of our culture.

Even the novelist of the seventies has emphasized the monotonous, self-indulgent message of "personal fulfillment." But this goal invariably surrenders to the emotional fact of narcissistic preoccupation which in its own way reinforces national impotence. Like the disco rhythm that inevitably converts all music into one sound, the contemporary novelist reduces all themes to self-appreciation and national powerlessness. When all relationships fail, when the support of traditional institutions are unavailable, all that remains is the self providing pleasures for its limitless delectation.

        With much serious artistic work demonstrating an obsession with technique, culture cannot easily navigate the straits between self-indulgence and social needs. The effect of this cultural battering is not benign. What has emerged is an apocalyptic view of society that suggests decline. The future, which was once filled with opportunity, is now characterized as riddled with insoluble problems. This, it seems to me, is our recent cultural legacy. The vitality needed to restore a positive vision of the future is the same vitality so sorely lacking in the arts and in politics. At this time it is not exaggerated to suggest that hope and cultural vitality are on the wane while a myth of impotence has appeared to replace them.

ABOUT "OTHERS" . . .

Chapter 12

Myth of World Community

"[The world is] a place on which England is found."
                                        G. K. Chesterton

"**A** myth," someone has said, "is a story that everyone accepts but no one believes."

The myth of the World State won acceptance a long time ago. If you trace the idea back to St. Augustine's *City of God,* it is 1500 years old; to Dante's *On World Government,* 500 years old. The myth is most appealing in times of extreme international turmoil — as in the above two cases, the first at the time Rome fell to the barbarians, the second when the church-state struggle had become intolerable. The most recent recrudescence of the World State idea took place after the bloodiest war to date, World War II, when the World Federalist movement, along with many others, got underway. In our present era of tension and Doomsday expectations of World War III, the notion of World Government or World Order is very much alive. In the summer of 1979, for example, Western Europe's first step toward a multinational assembly and government was made in the form of elections, something called the European Parliamentary Assembly. Too, the "nation-state" has fallen on hard times. To a number of modern political scientists, the nation-state has outlived its time; it promotes "nationalism," they claim, even fascism and the so-called "military-industrial complex"; it has become archaic and encrusted. Overheard on an elevator in a classroom building on an Eastern campus during the winter Olympics of 1980: "All those flags waving at the ceremonies. Ridiculous! Just another example of useless nationalism, 'my country right or wrong.'"

Given the obvious rationality and acceptability of the myth, why does the notion of World State nevertheless pass all belief? Has its fate been deserved?

The myth of World State clearly is an example of a fiction that is as useless as it is dangerous. That it has won wide acceptance today — in a time of virulent nationalism, separatism, and the breakup of empires — only mocks the concept and exposes its irrationality. There could be no worse time for a World State, or "internationalism," than now. The ash-can of history, to use Trotsky's term, is full of the debris left behind by the collapse of the British Empire (especially in its East-of-Suez extension), of the Portuguese Empire, of CENTO and SEATO alliances, of the "eternal" Sino-Soviet axis, of the United Arab Republic (the union of Egypt and Syria), etc. The future undoubtedly will bring more fractures — e.g., Scotland's separation from the United Kingdom, Quebec from Canada, and so on.

Besides being useless, the idea of World State and Internationalism presents dangers when it is taken seriously. Few World Federalists, I think, have ever taken the concept down to the wire and asked themselves serious, realistic questions about it. World State enthusiasts talk about a World Parliament, World Court, and the demise of nationalism and the national-sovereignty idea without realizing the consequences of their beliefs. Anyone who dares disagree with them looks like a raving chauvinist. Translate their idea into the reality of today's world. Around 170 nations send delegates to a World Assembly that has the prerogatives of a U.S. Congress or a British Parliament. The Assembly passes laws on taxation, defense, and other legislation that assures appropriations; it supervises appointments in the executive branch and on the World Court. It maintains and uses a World Army.

All of these decisions are by majority vote. That means that the small and medium-size states in the world dominate the World Assembly. In their taxation and appropriations, they rely on "contributions" from the better-off, industrial states that number only about 15 nation states, including the wealthiest one, the United States representing a mere 7% of the world's population. The revenues contributed in weighty amounts from the industrial states are used for welfare and defense programs devised by the majority of nations in Africa and Asia, countries that are part of the 2/3rds majority of subsistence or below-subsistence nation-states and whose birth rate and retarded economic development would devour the great burden of revenues.

One immediate result: precipitous declines in the standard of living of the industrial nations. Another: use of funds to serve the majority interests, with the danger that this could assume a punitive, military form so that industrial nations, ironically, would contribute to their own worst interests. Since most World Federalists live, guiltily, in the better-educated and well-off nations, one wonders how readily they would accept the punishing assaults against the home nation and its economic viability. Augustine's plaint against the "piratical" tendencies of princes in his own time would look exaggerated when compared to the massive plundering that would ensue were world-governmental decisions made by the majority of the world's nations!

Some people look at the United Nations institutions today as seeds for germinating the World State. The World Court, the General Assembly, the Security Council — aren't these forerunners? Not really. The first two have no "teeth" while the third is nothing but a place for tabulating the decisions already reached in the capitals of the five Permanent Members of the Council: China, Russia, Britain, France, and America. Moreover, for a court to be truly effective, it must have compulsory jurisdiction and adjudication. That is, its legal authority must be binding in the territorial sense; laying-on-of-hands (manus injectio), or going to court and standing trial and being sentenced, must also be binding. But the World Court has neither of these. It is like a doctor who lacks the power to write prescriptions, or even if he did write them, could not get them filled at the drugstore. Cases are submitted to the World Court only when disputing nations decide to submit them for adjudication. As to the General Assembly, none of its voted decisions have any substance. They are little more than pontifications to which a majority of nations may subscribe. It is probably not worth noting that the G.A. does not even represent all nations of the world, for its membership totals 151.

As to the concept, or vision, of "Internationalism," this is the Marxist-Leninist updating of the third of the famous French Revolution triad, "fraternity" — on a world scale. In the Communist vision, the "workers' solidarity" unites all nations.

The Soviet gloss on this Marxist idea adds: All roads lead to Moscow, the "Third Rome." Thus, in the Kremlin's version, Internationalism constitutes the following (in Brezhnev's words):

"Under contemporary conditions, the idea of Internationalism takes on an ever-increasing universal character . . . The forces of peace and social progress, and of social renewal, are growing stronger as they continue their victorious march throughout our planet!"

And, on the pattern of the "Internationalism" represented by the "Commonwealth" of some 20 Soviet Bloc and client-states worldwide all doing Moscow's bidding in one form or another (again, Brezhnev):

"This we definitely know: The cause for which the Motherland of the October Revolution struggles in the world arena will achieve victory!"

Premier Alexei Kosygin, as quoted by the Philippines First Lady, Mrs. Imelda Marcos, in *Newsweek*:

"Russia and its allies will control the high seas, space, and most of the world's landmass by the early 1980's."

As starts on the road to the World State, the institutions nestled at Turtle Bay, New York, are headed in the wrong direction. But one might ask: Why even head for World Government when it is unfeasible? Given the 170 or so sovereign states with their sovereign interests, what is the point in assuming that a consensus among them could ever arise and if it did, whether institutionalizing the consensus, by restricting sovereignties, would be the preferred course?

Kennedy, even in his most idealistic mood, could never have uttered such nonsense as, "Do not ask what the *world* can do for you but what you can do for the world." Loyalty ripples outwards like concentric circles. The innermost circle of loyalty is our family and closest friends; for them, we would do almost anything, maybe not even report them to the police or the CIA if they committed a crime, treason, or whatever. The next loyalty circle probably extends to neighborhood, city, state, maybe even country; we root for the "home-team," whether in the major leagues or at the Olympics; in a "just" war, we support our boys, our side. But in peacetime, the concentric circle of patriotic feeling for the homeland is weak, which may account for the sometime virulence of the World State idea in times of relative peace. When we go all the way to the outermost ring — The World — we find the weakest force of attraction of all: Centripetal forces, drawing loyalties outwards to the World State and

World Citizenship. The "World" is, in fact, a phantom, despite those clear, totalistic views of it caught by orbiting astronauts from their spaceship windows.

World Federalists, and Internationalists, use the term, "international community." This is another of their harmful assumptions, for there just is no such community. What, indeed, is a community? It is made up of people who have dwelled *together* for generations, who speak the same language, who recognize the same values and taboos, and who agree to disagree without doing violence to those who disagree. Put another way, a community is made up of people who are prepared to submit to a common judge, known as government. They are ready to submit because cohabitation has led to habituation, to a common allegiance to customs and traditions, to a common political culture. Until the world becomes a true community — which, ipso facto, is an impossibility, even a paradox — it would be most foolish to assume that disparate nations and their particular histories constitute anything so "organic."

Frankly, what we must do is discard the very metaphor of organism, as applied to the world and replace it with the metaphor of a chain. As the expression goes, a chain is as strong as its links. On the globe, the "links" are nations; the chain, the collectivity of nations. How do links get strengthened? Surely not by denying existence of the chain or by assuming communal organism. The best route, in fact, is the nationalistic one.

Now, nationalism has been given a very bad name by historians, most of whom choose World War I as their frame of reference. With the emotive suggestion of "gnash," in the first syllable of nationalism, the sound of the word and concept have come to connote something evil, synonymous with chauvinism and imperialism. Few historians have appreciated positive nationalism. In fact, there is no word in English, apparently, for healthy pride of nation that we normally associate with, say, budding national independence. E.g., both Philippine independence (from the United States) in 1946, Indian independence (from Britain) in 1947 unleashed a wave of national pride in those two places just as statehood for Israel in 1948. But who would scorn this species of healthy nationalism? Or, for that matter, our own nationalistic Era of Good Feelings — a very productive epoch — following the American Revolution and the War of 1812? Obviously, then, there are two, three, or more nationalisms.

Aristotle to the rescue: The Stagyrite, we trust, trained us to think of two opposite extremes, with a Golden Mean at mid-point. Thus, in the case of "lavishness" *versus* "stinginess," both are extremes; but something called "generosity" occupies the median. Likewise, at one extreme lies chauvinism — a love of country that is short-sighted and hateful because it preaches xenophobic scorn of other nations. At the other extreme lies isolationism — a prissy, anal-retentive view that regards the nation as so preciously perfect that it had best cut itself off from all intercourse worldwide. (Washington, in his Farewell Address, unintentionally displayed this excessive withdrawal syndrome.) Meanwhile, in the middle is plenty of room for *temperate* love of country — patriotism, even nationalism of the type that reflects affection for a nation's culture, for its contributions to other civilizations — a sound sense of concern over the nation's security in a world of weak international law and nonexistent legal sanctions. Such patriotism and nationalism blossom forth unnoticed in times of war, or, as I have indicated, at times of nation-building or founding.

Today, in the United States, patriotism has a bad name while nationalism gnashes on the ears. Why is this so? Too much peace? That would sound like the militarist philosophy of a von Treitzschke. Peace is welcome, especially in the Thermonuclear Age. But peace, as nice as it is to have around, is also — like everything else — a liability. Peace should not befuddle our judgement. To say, "Better Red than dead," for example, is to forget the healthy alternative: Better alive and free.

To protect Western freedom, political culture, and values — even with their faults — our feelings of protective pride of country are not out of place. Such feelings, however, cannot be manufactured, the way totalitarian states attempt to manufacture ersatz "enthusiasm" and "spontaneity," "patriotism" and "love for the Socialist Fatherland." In the West, the feelings either develop spontaneously or not at all. Still, it appears unwise to discourage them, as a number of laws and attitudes do. The useless, even harmful, World State myth is one of the forces that works against national unity, against the process by which links (nations) can become strong as the chain is strengthened. Notice that when links become weak — as in Korea in the late 1940's or in Vietnam in the early 1960's — such nations invite interference from outside. "Nature loves a vacuum," so other powers get tempted to move in. Even where nations display tremendous internal strength and patriotism, neighbors nevertheless may be tempted — but at their peril. This lesson was taught Israel's Arab neighbors in three wars. A population of over 3 million ferociously defended itself against a bloc representing well over 100 million. Would anyone deny that Israel achieved this feat, in large measure, because of her inner strength, her fierce love of country? Put another way, without Israeli pride, the three victories most likely would not have occurred.

To assume, then, that the world is on the brink of becoming a "World Community" is to operate with a premise that could lead to the direst of consequences for the very nations in which this communalist credo is popular. It leads to imagining a World Parliament into which each nation pours its sovereign rights. Shorn of these rights, the industrial nations prepare for their own surcease. The utopian scheme represented by World Federalism becomes a nightmare — Saturn consumes her own children. Above all, it implicitly devalues patriotism and nationalism.

An idea which is self-defeating ceases to be a useful myth; it becomes a nuisance. The false dichotomy of "international" *versus* "national" is created.

Any attempt to skip from the chain-linkage idea to a prematurely organismic conception only produces a Frankenstein's monster — man-made, but unnatural; huge, but unmanageable; towering, but at the same time menacing.

The French phrased the problem with customary Gallic clarity and candor when in their official April 1979 statement on the eve of the newly-born European Parliamentary Assembly, they said: "The election of the European Parliamentary Assembly must not result in an increase in its power." It won't. Then the statement added, obliquely: The Assembly will "formulate recommendations." Yes, that it will do.

Another French spokesman, Raymond Aron, summed it all up in this observation:

"Realism — the recognition of national selfishness — is more conductive to an awareness, on everyone's part, of the interests and ideas of others than idealism or the cult of abstract principles . . . Units larger than [a nation-stage] are ambiguous, never visible on the map, scarcely real in men's awareness."

Chapter 13

Myth of "MIC"

> "Civilization is distinguished from barbarism by the fact that
> the simple lie is replaced by a more complex one."
>
> Charles Fourier

During the Vietnam War, numbers of errant knights horsed themselves and took out after the dragon, the "military-industrial complex" (or MIC). Like dragons of yore, this one was, alas, only a figment of the imagination. Propagated enthusiastically by the same folk who bad-mouthed the war in Vietnam, these knights showed, by their compulsive passion to hyperbolize and conjure up specters, that the "complex" of which they spoke was none other than a psychic complex festering in their own minds.

The Heilbroners, Galbraiths, Melmans, Lapps, *et al.*, sometimes proudly referred to the originator of the expression, "military-indsutrial complex," that is, to President Dwight D. Eisenhower. What they did not point out, however, was that they had conveniently omitted an important phrase that Ike had inserted after the one quoted by the dragon-slayers. The oft-quoted line, of course, read, "We must guard against the acquisition of unwarranted influence . . . by the military-industrial complex." (Note that President, when he made this remark in his Farewell Address in 1961, had not said that the "complex" had *already* acquired such "unwarranted influence.") But after this, Ike then said:

"A vital element in keeping the peace is our Military Establishment. Our arms must be mighty, ready for instant action, so that no potential aggressor may be tempted to risk his own destruction . . . An alert and knowledgeable citizenry can compel the proper meshing of the huge industrial and military machinery of defense with our peaceful methods and goals so that security and liberty may prosper together."

Little is heard today from these knights who once rode herd through the pages of *Esquire, The Village Voice,* the *New York Review of Books, Rolling Stone,* or the Op-Ed page of *The New York Times.* Are they quiet now because the chimerical dragon has done a Chesire Cat and faded out of sight? Evidently it has, for our arms today are scarcely "mighty, ready for instant action, so that no potential aggressor may be tempted . . . etc." The level of our arms, and the expenditures on them, has been steadily declining, along parameters of either quality or quantity or both, since the mid-1960's (the Soviets and their States-side abettors distort the figures for these expenditures by intentionally ignoring the factor of inflation, which artificially prices-up our expenditures to "all-time highs"). Not only that, the "unwarranted influence" has reached a point where so few people volunteer today to serve in the armed forces that the country may be forced soon to resort to the draft in order to keep a bare minimum of soldiers on the ready and with sufficient training. The "influence" is so "great" that the appropriations for modernizing, say, our navy or acquiring a much-needed modern long-range bomber (e.g., the B-1) are blocked, either at the Administration level or farther down the line in the Congress (although the political barometers of the latter are only now beginning to register "Stormy" in the sense that storm-signals are revealing weaknesses in this nation's defenses).

The anti-MIC knights were not always so silent. Robert Heilbroner once told us that a "second political economy" exists in our country and which functions as "the industrial core of the primary industrial system." This "core," he said, is the defense industry. Mr. Heilbroner did not bother to tell the American public, nor did any of the other dragon-slayers, that only 4% of the total goods and services produced in this country in 1965-70, or about $40 billion, went into actual procurement of weapons. That leaves, I believe, 96% of the economy that was engaged in producing food, cigarettes, consumer goods like autos, refrigerators, or cosmetics — in other words, they made up the real "core" of our economy. The U.S. economy, obviously, is overwhelmingly non-defense oriented — over 9/10ths in fact — in regard to all aspects of economic activity, expenditures, consumption, investment, etc.

After reading dozens of articles taking the anti-MIC line, I finally decided in the late 'sixties to look into the whole matter on my own. I must say that I had absolutely no axe to grind, beyond a suspicion that I, like others, was being taken in. I recalled, as I began my research, that anti-MIC publicists were claiming that the "most important part of Big Business" was directly involved in defense contracts. Just how, I wondered, *was* that $40 billion divided among companies producing military hardware? Was a major share of corporate Big Business involved in arms-making? Was that "Mr. Businessman," who was depicted by charts-happy songwriters as a totally heartless, sinister figure, hauling in colossal profits by making weapons? It seemed strange to me, with 96% of American business in peaceful-type production, that very many of Mr. Businessman's activities could possibly include making arms (by the looks of our arms today, I would guess, retrospectively, too little).

What I found, in a nutshell, was that the nation's defense business was divided up among no less than 20,000 firms! True, some of these took the lion's share of the defense orders — they were, obviously, the aerospace companies. But as to the assertion that "giant corporations" were making huge profits off weapons, I found to be as fictitious as the dragon itself. For example, among the top ten companies in terms of the defense business they did in the years 1965-70, were such well-known ones as General Electric, General Dynamics, and American Telephone & Telegraph Company. But when you looked at the "mix" of their profits, generally small shares of them came from doing defense business (with the exception of General Dynamics, 67% of whose business in those years, was defense-oriented). In the cases of General Electric, which was No. 5 on the defense-maker list, and A. T. & T., which was No. 8, only 19% and 9% respectively of their profits came from defense contracts. The same picture showed up for the large corporations up and down the list: Their business was overwhelmingly non-defense oriented.

Which companies, then, preoccupied themselves mainly with defense business? Well, these were Lockheed,

88% of whose assets were derived from defense business, McDonnell-Douglas, with 75%, North-American Rockwell, 57%. In other words, the aerospace companies — *in those years* but not so much today by any means — were deeply involved in producing military hardware, and, by the way, accounting for whatever strength in arms that our country enjoys today. But aerospace companies are not huge; most of them are medium-size. In fact, a pair of otherwise anti-MIC authors were obliged to admit this. In *The Pentagon Watchers*, p. 227, where Rodberg and Shearer said: "Medium-size corporations receive the largest share of defense contracts." Despite the facts, however, the anti-MIC knights went right on hammering away at the public that most of Big Business was in a "conspiracy" with the Pentagon to sell as many arms as possible, at public expense.

Another whipping-boy of the knights-errant was their false allegation that a "large share" of America's labor force was engaged in defense production. Not being satisfied to distort the truth concerning dollars and cents, the anti-MIC crowd began to clamor that the bulk of our skilled and unskilled workers, and technical people, were caught up in the "web" of producing weapons. Even *Time* magazine unwittingly got into the act, with an embarrassing pair of statistical errors.

Time's researchers are justifiably regarded as careful sleuths, past whom few errors make it into print. "Checkers" are notorious gad-flies that buzz around the editors' typewriters. And yet, this horror managed to sneak by them (in the April 11, 1969, issue): "According to a recent estimate, 21% of skilled bluecollar workers and 16% of professional employees are on the payrolls that rely on military spending." Astounding, I thought. Fully a fifth of our skilled blue-collars and 16% of our "technical" employees are helping turn out weapons! But when I tracked down the source of these figures — the *Statistical Abstract of the United States* — found that *Time* had jumbled the facts. The *Time* sentence should have read, as the *Statistical Abstract* had:

"Twenty-one per cent *of the total labor force employed in defense-related industries* are skilled bluecollar workers."

A quite different proposition from what *Time* had said! As to the professional, or technical, employees, the *Statistical Abstract* read as follows:

"Sixteen per cent *of all those engaged in defense work* were classed as professional."

Again, a gremlin had apparently crept into the checker desks at *Time*. (No one wrote, or, at least, published, a letter in *Time* about the error, and I discovered it too late to get my two-cents' worth in.)

The bottom line of all this is that only a very small part of the entire U.S. working force, whether white or blue-collar, skilled or unskilled or professional, was — or especially today is — engaged in defense-related work. In the peak Vietnam War years, a labor force of about 3 million was estimated by the U.S. Department of Labor as being directly employed in defense-hardware production. This represented a mere 3-4% of the total national labor pool of 80 million men and women. And yet none of these, and the other facts that I have recounted above, deterred CBS in the slightest when it cooked up a "Special" about "militarism in American life." I examined this scenario for a program that was aired in the late 'sixties; it was biased and mythic from the first to the last utterance. In retrospect, the "red network" is probably not particularly proud of it.

Another famous victim of the MIC dragon-hunters was the alleged "defense-rich" states of the Union. Senators and Congressmen from such states were depicted as corruptible and corrupted toadies who could be easily induced to feather the nests of their own constituencies by supporting pork-barrel appropriations for weapons procurement that was good business for their home states. A "hawk" became a hawk simply because showing of talons pleased the arms-makers back home. I said to myself, whenever I read such insinuations, if they are true, then Ike must be right that constant vigilance about the spreading influence from the Pentagon is necessary. But I also told myself, if such tales are untrue, I hope that the next Senator or Congressman, so accused, will bop the accusers on the nose! (I later heard that Sen. "Scoop" Jackson, of Washington State, home of Boeing, was tempted into such reactions when so provoked by irresponsible accusers, as he frequently was in those years.)

When I tracked down this accusation against Congress and the legislative heart of the nation, the very principles of representative democracy and the way they function here, I became even more surprised than I was when I unraveled the other anti-MIC claims and innuendoes. For what I found was that those states that did the *most defense business* had actually sent to the Senate and the House a *proportionately greater number of outstanding doves!* There were more doves than hawks in their own midsts, I found, and more doves sent by them to the Capitol than were sent by states doing less defense business! In a few cases, true, congressmen, from areas containing defense installations — in the form of army, navy, or air force bases or other facilities — tended to vote more "hawkish" when it concerned *that particular installation* — i.e., they supported appropriations to continue the given base or facility. But in some cases, even they voted dovish on certain national issues — as, e.g., defense appropriations of certain types, on the issue of whether an SST should be built at government expense, and so on.

"Pressures exerted by powerful corporations are felt in the Pentagon, in the White House, and are reflected in Congress . . . Few Congressmen care to challenge defense expenditures." So wrote Ralph Lapp in his reckless and harmful book entitled, *The Weapons Culture.* But another, somewhat lukewarm as well as flustered anti-Pentagon writer, Bruce Russett, had to admit, in *What Price Vigilance* that, "It is striking how little our expectations (of hawkish voting by defense-rich states) are borne out. DoD prime contract awards show absolutely *no* relationship to *any* (Russett's emphasis) of the . . . scales of Senate voting" (established for the purpose of measuring alleged MIC influence on Senatorial voting).

The *Congressional Quarterly Almanac,* the highly respected, unbiased source of Congressional voting patterns, and a highly respected journal among political scientists of whatever stripe, made a thorough-going study of defense voting in Congress in 1969. The CQA Capitol-watchers found that differences in voting on defense-related issues divided Senators and Congressmen by their views — conservative, liberal, middle-of-theroad — not by state. Meanwhile, some of the most outspoken of Solon-doves, noted CQA, came from dove-cote states that were uncommonly rich in defense contracts! California, New York, Pennsylvania, Ohio — or Nos. 1, 3, 5, and 7 among the top ten states in amount of defense business (1969) — sent such people to the Congress as Representatives Ryan and Cohelan, or Senators Cranston and Goodell. According to CQA, "the most prominent figures [advocating reduced military expenditures]" included: William S. Moorhead (D, PA); Richard D. McCarthy (D, NY); Otis G. Pike (D, NY); Lucien N. Nedzi (D, MI); Robert L. Legget (D. CA); Robert T. Stafford (R, VT); and Charles W. Whalen, Jr. (R, OH). Most of these states, from which these Congressmen originated, were among the top ten, either in dollar-amounts of their defense business or by the percent of the state's labor force — which in all cases was insignificant — engaged in defense-related production.

The only state that was an exception in this pattern of doves-from-defense-rich-states was Texas. The Lone Star State was No. 2 on the defense-business and labor-force lists, but it is hard to agree that Texans vote hawkishly, as they tend to, merely because of the defense business located in their state. (At least, it is not advisable to make the accusation of venality to a Texan's face!) In any case, only 15% of the total state's gross product of goods and services measured in dollars and cents was derived from defense contracts in the war years. Instead of the venality factor, some analysts argue that traditional Texan conservatism about national security, pride of country, "pepper & vinegar," and some other typically Texan ingredients are at work here. They back up their argument by pointing to the generally pro-defense voting pattern of the South as a whole (most Southern states, however, have a very tiny share of national-defense business).

In pondering the motives of those who are so ready to cast aspersions on our representative system of democracy and capitalism, one cannot ignore the socialist-ideological biases to which some, at least, of the dragon-hunting knights have openly admitted. A socialist, after all, has only the weakest of loyalties to representative democracy under capitalism. He believes in knee-jerk fashion that the capitalist system determines the opinions of all "vested interests" related to that system — only money talks, not individual Senators or Congressmen, or for that matter, average citizens and voters.

Above all, the socialist-leaning, or -committed, anti-capitalist believes that capitalism breeds war. This notion has at long last become the darling of some of the most commonly-used textbooks on U.S. college campuses today — and, so, by the way, has the "Pentagon-capitalism" myth.

"As in Facist Italy or Nazi Germany," claimed the authors of *The Pentagon Watchers,* "the work of the state [in the U.S.] becomes the making of war." By joining this argument to that of the Heilbroners, Melmans, C. Wright Millses, and Galbraiths, that American Big Business breeds defense contracts and that the "core" of American corporate business is rooted in arms-making — all pernicious myths — you get the following crypto-Marxist Communist line: "America is a warmonger because it does most of its business from making and using weapons against other countries."

Long before Marx and Lenin gave prominence to the myth about arms-makers causing war, a vulgate version of why wars happen had been taken up by uninitiated or outright illiterate, semi-paranoid members of society. "Merchants of death," said such folk, start wars by convincing civilian political leaders of the existence of imaginary enemies; "war profiteering" leads to political log-rolling and the pork barrel which in turn entice Presidents and Congressmen into military adventures. Yet, when you look into history, with an unbiased eye, you find that it is not arms, generals, or arms-makers that cause war, only civilian policymakers with war on their minds — for expansionistic, ideological, or for some other reasons, most of which are only rarely economic in origin. As it turns out — say, in the case of Imperial Germany, Hitler Germany, or Imperial Japan in the 1930's — the aggressive intent came first, the arms second, and war came when the arms matched the intent. When this happened, the unarmed had to make all haste to survive.

Powerful nations have become aggressive because they felt their power; the weakly-armed duly became their victims. Is it necessary to cite Poland in 1939, South Korea in 1950, South Vietnam in 1964, Somalia in 1979? How could Marx's rule — about economic or "imperialist" prompting of war based on arms-making profiteering — possibly apply to these countries? In fact, take every one of the major wars of this century and you see that the profiteering role of business (that is, where you can find it) had nothing whatever to do with the starting of the wars. What business did, actually, was to fulfill its industrial role after the wars were well underway. Who would believe that American business "engineered" Hitler's march into Austria, Poland, France, or for that matter Soviet Russia? Was Pearl Harbor caused by "American imperialism"? Did Russia invade Finland in 1939 because of "capitalist-imperialist greed"? Or take the case of World War I for example. President Wilson asked Congress for a declaration of war against the Kaiser precisely at the time when American Big Business was least able or willing to cope with war. Later, we were hit in Korea when we were pulling down our fences. As to Vietnam, that war was incredibly unprofitable to most of Big Business.

And in the 1970's and '80's, the world is beset by inter-Communist-state wars — as in Southeast Asia, where a power-hungry Communist Vietnam seeks to establish hegemony over that strategic transit point through the Afro-Asian Ocean, to use the geopolitical term for the water routes found in the Pacific and Indian Oceans leading to resource-rich areas in the Near and Middle East. Are we to believe that capitalists are responsible for such Vietnamese toppling of Southeast Asian dominoes?

Leonard Silk, of *The New York Times,* once spelled out this unprofitability of war to capitalists — and the Vietnam War in particular — by quoting an analysis made by Northwestern University economist, Professor Robert Eisner, who showed that American business actually lost $113.4 billion in five years of the war at its height. This didn't include lost business opportunity — the cost of shifting resources away from normal and better-paid activities into government-subsidized defense, which is considerably less profitable when compared to free-market-derived profits. Eisner calculated that the men who were conscripted would have earned $82.5 billion more at home, and have been that much more of a market for our peace-oriented business. Moreover, Silk's figures showed that corporations' profits fell by 16.8% between 1965 and 1970; in the five previous years, they had been rising to the tune of 61.2%. The value of corporate stocks fell by 36.5% from 1965 to 1970, while they had been rising 48.5% in the five previous years.

By just about any index, the Vietnam War was undeniably unprofitable — taking the nation's economy as a whole. As for the aerospace companies that were deeply involved in defense contracts in those years, even for them the profit margins were far less than they would have been had the civilian free market been their garden. Not surprisingly, Standard & Poor's business profiles of these companies stressed the greater profitability of non-defense, non-governmental business; prices of aviation stocks for the most part trended downward during much of the war. Stockholders are obviously aware of the greater leverage provided by the hunting ground of the free market. (Since the war, aerospace firms for the most part have been busy making civilian aircraft designed for carrying tour-bound passengers throughout the country and the world.)

Finding the causes for war is a far more arduous task than the simple-minded "Pentagon-watchers," Naderites, or outright Marxist-Leninists depict it to be. Anyone who has studied, say, Australian Professor Geoffrey Blainey's excellent book, *The Causes of War*, knows how falsely mythical it is to imagine that countries go to war merely or even mainly for economic reasons. As Blainey demonstrates, the economic or "economic-imperialist" cause of war is grossly exaggerated. Arthur Koestler has said that modern wars are more likely to occur over "semantic space" — for the goals of ideology — than for physical space, or territory. Nor, for that matter, is the naked-ape argument convincing — that man's savage-animal past haunts him even today and makes him warlike. This is not convincing for at least two reasons: 1) animals get along better with each other than humans do with each other; 2) belligerency is not known to be carried in the genes.

No, wars cannot be derived from economic or genetic determinism, or "programming." But there is a very potent source of war, particularly in the 20th century. In the form of myth and reality, it stalks the world right now. About that in the following chapters.

Chapter 14

Myth of Ideology

"The only choice is either bourgeois or Socialist ideology. There is no middle course (for mankind has created no 'third' ideology), nor, moreover, in a society torn by class antagonisms can there ever be a non-class or above-class ideology."

V. I. Lenin

"Mankind lives, and will live in the future, according to the teachings of Marx, Engels, and Lenin, whose ideas remain immortal."

L. I. Brezhnev

"**T**hinking makes it so," runs the old saw. Put more fancily, attitudes, myths, political programs, and goals may become self-fulfilling prophecies. For example, if I persist in relating to people on the basis of the (useful) myth that faith, hope and charity are what make, or should make, the world turn round, is it totally unlikely that I will stimulate faith, hope and charity in others? Reverse the phrase to read: faithlessness, despair, and hatred. Suppose on the basis of this (pernicious) myth-assumption I relate to other people. Isn't it likely that I will get all these negative non-values thrown right back in my face?

Now, there is no guarantee that the trinity of good-will is going to create that ideal world. But it's for damned sure that the triad of hatred won't.

The same applies to the famous saying, "The ends justify the means." If I regard my goals as so sacred that I am permitted to employ even the most dire means to realize them — including, say, armed terrorism — what may happen to those remote goals? I may never reach them; no one may be around to "enjoy" the ultimate "paradise." The fact is that the ends and the means work in tandem with each other and cannot be separated. In other words, en route to reaching our goals, we should practice those means which are in the spirit of the goals. Otherwise, we may never reach them, or become so corrupted in the process of attaining them by the sordid means that we employ that the goals become pie in the sky.

Neither of these truisms about myth — the self-prophesying action nor the ends-and-means problem — have sunk in for the great majority of mankind, or surely for the overwhelming majority of today's political leaders. The world is too amply populated with political leaders who prophesy doom and destruction, mutual suspicion and hatred, struggle and war, and who believe in using any and all means to forward their political designs. Unhappily, the stigma and curse upon our century is precisely this confused sense of value.

This century opened with a world historical political event which utterly changed the world and the "rules" by which the game of international politics would in future be played. The event was the Communist take-over in Russia in November 1917, mistakenly called a "revolution."

Harvard Professor Adam Ulam put it well, in his contribution to the Kurt London volume, *The Soviet Impact on World Politics* (1974), when he pointed out that a whole new era in modern history was ushered in by the Leninist *coup d'etat*. It brought with it the uncompromising, totalistic nature of the Communist ideology, its denial of "bourgeois norms" of international behavior (which had kept the 19th century relatively peaceful compared to its predecessors), above all, its Machiavellian attitude toward ends and means — or as Lenin put it, "using all means, lying if necessary" in order to make the rest of the world in the Soviet image.

Marxism-Leninism, however, did more than recommend hypocrisy; it advocated brute force in order to help the "inevitable" process of history move in the prescribed, "deterministic" direction. In Ulam's view, and you can't help but agree with him, Soviet immoral behavior actually abetted the rise of Hitler in Germany: "The breakdown of the general principles of international obligation and the norms of international comity, which had occurred before and largely because of the USSR," Ulam wrote, contributed to Hitler's success. Hitler's territorial claims, based on Lebensraum and the existence of German minorities in foreign territories "were no more shocking than those advanced by the Soviet Union by virtue of its role as the Fatherland of Socialism."

Both Hitler and Mussolini admitted, on various occasions, that they had learned a good deal about revolutionary politics and diplomacy, and the astute use of propaganda with which, by myths, to mislead the masses and the intelligentsia, from the "Jewish Bolsheviks." (Relatively few Jews were among the top Bolsheviks.) In *Table Talks,* der Führer explicitly states that his National Socialists, with their flaming-red banners, their party cells, "party-mindedness" (in Russian, *partiinost'*), etc., copied their "organizational techniques" from the Russian Bolsheviks. The same can be said of Lenin's, Stalin's and Brezhnev's labor camps; party-controlled media; "Agitprop," or agitation and propaganda; state-controlled labor unions; purges; party-controlled military; heroic totalitarian art, whether as paintings or posters; use of films to arouse patriotic fervor; paramilitary organizations; above all, double-dealing in international politics. No wonder that Mussolini once dubbed Stalin a "crypto-Fascist."

The debt owed by Fascism to the Marxist-Leninist totalitarians was, indeed, enormous. But there was one other aspect of the Communist system, especially as it was exhibited under Stalin — as it turned out, for a quarter of a century — that was suggestive to any Fascists or their successors, some of the latterday versions of whom renounce "Fascism" while nevertheless practicing a distinct form of it. This was the nationalistic Bolshevik concept of the "Chosen Class" within the "Chosen Nation." As a myth, it has proved incomparably explosive and danger-ridden. Today it acts as a self-fulfilling prophecy with the most lethal consequences for the rest of the world.

It was Lenin who said, boldly and without a trace of hesitation or qualification: "The Russian proletariat [is] the vanguard of the international proletariat." It was left to Stalin to refine this racist-sounding doctrine into the Stalin toast lifted to the Great Russian people after World War II: "I would like to drink to the health of our Soviet people and, above all, to the Great Russian people because it is the most outstanding nation of all the nations located in the Soviet Union . . . It is the leading people [in the world] because it has clear mind, firm character, and endurance."

"It" has a "clear mind . . . etc."? The Great-Russian Staatsvolk, of the USSR, increasingly gets this kind of racist praise today, not only from Soviet leaders, but from over 80 Soviet-aligned Communist Party Fifth Columns distributed throughout the world, and from some 80 more underground apparats or crypto-Communist "front" organizations in countries that outlaw the Party or in which Maoist-type CPs predominate. At the latest Soviet Party congress, in 1976, one foreign Communist after the other described the USSR as the Chosen Nation to lead the world in the Soviet direction — that is, toward all those totalitarian lovelies we've heard so much about, from the brave Solzhenitsyns, Sakharovs, Bukovskys, and Shcharanskys.

Such Chosen-Nation messianism is dangerous enough, in a world that includes the political-military means with which to attain the ends, in the form of thermonuclear weapons. (Lenin once recommended that Communists must be ready to use the "most lethal weapons," if necessary, in order to spread the system.) But when the Marxist-Leninist ideology is added to the volatile mixture of Great-Russian hegemonism, the self-fulfilling aspect looms like a mushroom-shaped cloud on the horizon.

It all goes back to Marx, in the sense that this "Holy Ghost" of the creed laid such stress on the factor of violence with which to reach communist society. Brute force, said Marx, is the mid-wife of historical change; it has always been this way and will continue to be in the future; it is, he said, "inevitable."

Lenin went even farther than this, finding and describing all sorts of struggles, national-liberation wars, guerrilla warfare, etc., as absolutely necessary to The Cause.

Lenin: "We have never rejected terror nor can we do so . . . Killing of individuals, such as high officials and lower-ranking members of the police and of the army [may be necessary]."

Lenin: "No Marxist should consider warfare . . . as immoral or demoralizing . . . Guerrilla warfare should be ennobled by the enlightening and organizing influence of Socialism."

Brezhnev: "The last decisive battle for the overthrow of capitalism and for Socialism draws near."

Brezhnev: "We are not pacifists. We are not in favor of peace at any price, nor of course, are we for any freezing of social and economic processes which take place inside countries . . . The kind of peace we understand is that which was given to the heroic Vietnamese people, its historic victory waged in the struggle against imperialist aggression.''

The Soviets, like their ideological friends throughout the world, are clearly obsessed with forcible "historical change." Most recently, they have made this quite obvious in their use of brute force, in order to achieve Socialist ends, in Korea, Vietnam, Laos, Cambodia, Angola, Ethiopia, Somalia, the Yemens, Zaire, Afghanistan. Bullets instead of ballots, class struggle instead of multi-class cooperation, force instead of patient persuasion or compromise: these are the Soviet preferences and the methods that have scarred the face of this century, creasing it with the mark of Cain.

"Sincere diplomacy," said Stalin, "is no more possible than dry water or wooden iron." Stalin went on, "Words must have no relation to actions — otherwise, what kind of diplomacy is it? Words are one thing, actions another." The Man of Steel in Moscow, and his successors, have broken over 100 treaties — according to an analysis made of the violations by a U.S. Senate Judiciary Committee study in 1959, after 38 years of Soviet existence and hundreds of friendship, nonaggression, etc., treaties made by the USSR with non-Communist countries. This is the evidence for how the Soviets and their diplomacy have flouted the "old norms" in the way Professor Ulam indicated. Communists should realize, said a recent ideological pronouncement out of Moscow, "that there is no morality *in general,* that there is no kindness or justice *in general.* There is only Communist morality which has nothing in common with bourgeois morality."

When certain types of Western intellectuals hear statements like the above, they are likely to react as follows: "Oh, that is merely Communist posturing. It's like a rain-dance, mere ritual. Why take it seriously?" This, more or less, has been the description made at various times of Marxism-Leninism, for example, by the late Erich Fromm, of *Escape from Freedom* and *The Art of Love* fame. But you hear it in many circles. These are often the same people who talk of "convergence" between Soviet-style Socialism and American capitalism. "There's not all that much difference, friend. In any case, we're becoming more like them, and they like us with every passing day." (This was — and is — a plank in the New Left program.) The Beatles even made a song out of it, when one of their lyrics lumped together the U.S. and U.S.S.R., playing on the initials of the similar-sounding but radically different countries.

Can ideas, myths, programs, goals be viewed merely as innocuous ritual, a litany which is sung but not believed? As one American Soviet specialist once asked ironically, is it possible that Brezhnev & Co., after finishing a diatribe on the wonders wrought by class struggle, "just war," national-liberation local wars, and Soviet-style Socialism in the USSR, and other such standbys in the Communist ideological treasure-trove, leave the rostrum and then mutter to the other comrades sitting on the dais, "Well, once again we gave 'em the old baloney." On the contrary, the Soviet leadership gives every indication that it believes fervently in what it says: that the world will eventually, rather soon in fact, go Socialist or be Socialist- (read Soviet-) dominated. Brezhnev has maintained on many occasions — quoting from Lenin and Stalin in the process — all assistance will be lent to the "world-revolutionary process": "We will follow our revolutionary conscience no matter where it may lead," Marshal and General Secretary Brezhnev told the XXVth Party Congress in 1976.

The notion that violent means, advocated in ideology, can be used legitimately to reach the sacred ends — of Socialism or "national-liberation" — has long since sunk into mentalities of a number of nations and leaderships represented within the United Nations, as the former U.S. Ambassador to the world body, Senator Daniel Patrick Moynihan, has shown in his various writings. I myself found evidence of the mentality when I was recently pursuing the U.N. position on transnational terrorism. In the view of a number of countries, largely of the more radical segment of the Arab Near East, terrorism happens "naturally," like the cue ball hitting the No. 3 ball at the proper angle so that it drops into the corner pocket. This "mechanist-deterministic" argument was neatly contained, I discovered, in UN G.A. Document A/C.6/32/L.13, Agenda Item 118, dated Dec. 1, 1977. To wit: "[Terrorism's] underlying causes lie in misery, frustration, grievance, and despair, and cause some people to sacrifice human lives, including their own, in an attempt to effect radical changes." Which "cause some people" — in other words, terrorists do not will their skyjackings and their murders and kidnappings; they are, as it were, forced into these actions by "misery, frustration, grievance . . . etc." As Stalin was fond of adding on occasion, "Clear, one would think." Here you have expressed in a succinct and candid manner the rationale for acts of terrorism: No one exactly wills them or can be blamed for the murders or whatever; these acts are "caused," amorphously, by circumstances. Also implied is the heroism of the terrorists' "attempt to effect radical changes." As though such changes, because they are "radical," are, ipso facto, good, necessary, "progressive."

Could anything be more wrongheaded . . . and dangerous?

Translated into foreign policy — that is, into Vietnams, Angolas, and Afghanistans — *applied* Soviet doctrine is clearly the world's No. 1 danger. And yet, not only in our own country but in many other nations of what used to be referred to as the Free World — which is shrinking by the year — the "Domesticrats" have taken over.

These are the people for example, who come on the air, with the evening news, which has been written for them by other Domesticrats, containing the message that the U.S. of A. has "so many problems of its own" that it scarcely has time to worry about the "Soviet threat," or whether a "Fifth Fleet" might be needed in the Indian Ocean, or whether it matters that our expenditures on defense and on Research & Development in the military field are declining (as a percentage of GNP) so that we are less able to keep up with the state of the art, as it is practiced by the other superpower, U.S.S.R. Foreign affairs, in other words, has tended to take second place on the "7 o'clock news" unless, of course, something dire or something unusually newsworthy occurs, such as the Begin-Sadat treaty-signing ceremony of 1978. But as to the ground swell of ideology underlying these events, and the geopolitical/geostrategic realities which basically influence the treaty signings, the assassinations of ambassadors and businessmen, and countless other deeds that earn top billing on the news — these determiners are relatively ignored.

The "correlation of forces throughout the world has shifted in the Socialist favor," reads today's updated ideology out of the Kremlin. "The offensive against the positions of imperialism is proving victorious," reads another.

Could be. But is it "inevitable"? By merely reiterating it, like a Hitlerian Big Lie, the Soviets hope that their intentions will become self-fulfilling. Ideology, in other words, is used, as the Marxist-Leninists put it, as a "weapon" — in this case, to get the world to thinking in the inevitable terms imbedded in the Kremlin's ideology. Plato's notion of a ruling myth, or Royal Lie, used not only to give bonding to society but to get it to thinking in certain predictable ways (as he explains it in two dialogs, *The Republic* and *The Statesman*) is clearly implied in the use made of ideology by the Soviets in their global campaign.

How are the Western democracies and their allies going to contend with the myth of ideology and the myths contained in Marxist-Leninist ideology? By inventing their own? Well, they already possess their own quiver of myth-arrows. Western liberal-democracy is replete with all sorts of mythic statements concerning equality, collective wisdom, representation of the popular will, free enterprise, and so on. A good many of these myths actively govern and prove effective in actual practice and daily life. What is missing is only the will to propagate our own myths. Or even to recognize them as "regulative ideas," to use Kant's term, whose validity rides upon their effectiveness in practice, even if their "noumenal" assumptions cannot be proved (nor can the assumptions of Marxism-Leninism be proved). In other words, we already have what Aristotle called a "wondrous tissue" of myth. Why don't we exhibit it?

Chapter 15

Myth of Peace

> "It is time to understand that peaceful coexistence extends to inner-*state* relations. It does not replace, nor could it replace, the laws of class struggle, of the national-liberation movement, and of social progress."
>
> *Pravda*, April 8, 1976

> "Our Country does not interfere in the internal affairs of the others countries and peoples. But we do not conceal our views. In the developing countries, as everywhere else, we stand by the forces of progress, democracy, and national independence."
>
> L. I. Brezhnev

"**W**orld War III has, in fact, begun."

These are not the words of a sci-fi writer or a Doomsday arm-chair strategist. They were uttered by a member of the Soviet Communist Party Central Committee. Yakov Malik made the assertion — quoted on the front page of The New York Times, February 3, 1952 — at the United Nations during the Korean War.

Malik's seven deliberately-chosen words contained more essential Marxism-Leninism, the basic principles underlying contemporary Soviet foreign policy and diplomacy, than all the verbiage produced about "peaceful coexistence" and the "relaxation of tensions (detente)" going all the way back to approximately 1920, when the two formulations were first announced by the Lenin regime.

The fact is that Soviet tactics and strategy are in complete harmony with Comrade Malik's statement. To the Russians, war and peace are not strictly separable. In the politics of peacetime, wrote Lenin, "the contours of war can be noticed in a disguised form." Vladimir Ilyich was fond of quoting the Prussian military strategist, Karl von Clausewitz (1780-1831), to the effect that "war is merely the continuation of politics by other means." The line separating war from peace and peace from war is a very thin one, say the Communists, as long as capitalism exists anywhere in the world. Until capitalism is "liquidated" worldwide, as all various shades of Marxist-Leninists maintain, the world remains in a twilight zone of "neither peace nor war," or as Soviet military writers put it, in a state of "perpetual preparation." Because there is no clear start of an "inter-class" world war, the preliminaries to any actual fullfledged war combine peaceful appearances with military designs. Lenin once said, "When we are strong enough, we shall take capitalism by the scruff of the neck." Until that time comes, something less than total peace, but also something less than all-out war, is the fate of the pre-Socialist world.

Leon Trotsky, Lenin's right-hand man, coined the expression, "neither peace nor war," to describe the situation in which the Soviet Republic found itself in 1918 after the "October Revolution," or Bolshevik seizure of power. But Trotsky confessed, in his memoirs, that this expression also applied to Soviet foreign policy in general — at any time, or until the "permanent revolution" overturning capitalism throughout the world had reached completion. Meantime, said Lenin, a series of "frightful clashes" await the world until Soviet-style Socialism reigns totally and in perpetuity. According to Yugoslav sources, there have been over 100 "frightful clashes" involving "Marxist struggle" since World War II.

Now, in the thermonuclear age, it might seem that Marxist-Leninists would revise these dangerous, pre-atomic ideas of Lenin, Trotsky, Stalin, *et al.* In fact, in 1956, at the 20th Party Congress, Nikita Khrushchev declared that the Lenin assertion about the *"fatal* inevitability" of world war, so long as capitalism exists, had become obsolete. Without quite saying the phrase was completely obsolete, Khrushchev at least disputed the word "fatally" in the inevitability-formula; by retaining any fatalism about World War III, Khrushchev and others explained, there was no point in exploiting the Peace Campaigns launched from Moscow, in the form of the Stockholm Peace sign-ins, demonstrations, manifestoes, etc. By making war seem more avoidable than inevitable, the Communists hoped to inject more energy into their peace movement — while still rejecting pacifism as the worst kind of nonsense.

Such partial revisions of Leninism aside, the creed, as interpreted in Moscow and not only there, still considers the peace that the world does have today — as long as capitalism exists anywhere on the globe — as calico-thin; neither-war-nor-peace. Worse, Soviety military and civilian writings depict the present precarious peace as a frame for continuation of the politics of armed revolutionary struggle for which peaceful coexistence and detente serve as convenient abettors rather than inhibitors. To wit:

"The pacifist program [is] a form of class struggle, a tactic used by the Socialist country in the struggle against the reactionary bourgeoisie" (Lenin).

"The policy of peaceful coexistence is a policy for mobilizing the masses and launching vigorous action against the enemies of peace. Peaceful coexistence of states does not imply renunciation of class struggle . . . The coexistence between states with differing social systems is a form of class struggle between Socialism and capitalism" (Statement of the 81 Communist and Workers' Parties, Moscow, 1960).

"The Soviet Union's pursuit of peace and friendship between nations [includes] the resolute struggle against imperialism [and] giving undeviating support to the peoples' struggles for democracy, national liberation, and Socialism" (Brezhnev).

"Our country does not interfere in the internal affairs of other countries and peoples. But we do not conceal our views. In the developing countries, as everywhere else, we stand by the side of the forces of progress, democracy, and national liberation. (Brezhnev).

"The Soviet Union sees in detente a means whereby more favorable conditions can be created for peaceful construction of Socialism and Communism. At the same time, it is unmistakably clear that detente in no way replaces, nor can it replace or change, the laws of class struggle" (*Pravda*, March 25, 1976).

What, then, is the positive content of peaceful coexistence-detente, in the Russian view? Is it merely camouflage for Soviet-backed or inspired national-liberation struggle, terrorism, Marxist take-overs in capitalist, or in semi-capitalist, or semi-socialist developing countries? Or can peace, even given the existence of capitalism somewhere in the world, become durable instead of a mere absence of actual world war? Malik says that World War III has already begun, but no H-bombs are falling: Can this ultimate stage of W.W. III be avoided?

Sad to say, a thorough examination of all types of Soviet writings — civilian or military, propagandistic or scholarly — turns up some pretty grim philosophy concerning the Kremlin's view of the atomic-age world as a possibly safe place in which to live. It's as though the leadership, from Lenin and Stalin to Khrushchev and Brezhnev, were looking out of Kremlin windows-on-the-world with the shades drawn. They have, in fact, cast the world in their own image, to paraphase a line from Nelson Goodman's *Ways of Worldmaking*. Like the cartographer, Mercator, they have in effect wrapped a cylinder of paper around the globe, laid it out in two dimensions upon a table, and then squeezed the four-dimensional earthly existence into a two-dimensional, Procrustean bed.

This Soviet World is nothing less than a two-sided battleground, or "arena," to use the common Soviet expression. In the arena a "world-historical" combat is today taking place, say the Russians. (Ironically, the prevailing view from Western windows-on-the-world is the exact opposite: No world-historical struggle, no "inevitable" historical process leading anywhere in particular. Only individual countries living four-dimensionally and going routinely about their business of getting and spending and laying waste their powers — nothing profound, nothing "Hegelian" at all . . .) For the Russian Communist leaders and ideologists, the USSR is the engineer of what Stalin called the "locomotive of history." In up-to-date writings out of Moscow, the "October Revolution" and the "true Socialism practiced in the Soviet Union" are compared in their historical importance to the birth of Christ or Martin Luther's Ninety-five Theses nailed to the Castle Church door in Wittenburg. As Trotsky put it: "The October Revolution must be regarded as the departure point for an entirely new history of mankind." According to Leonid Brezhnev's Collected Works, the Bolshevik take-over in Russia "is a watershed dividing all the forces of the Old World . . . from the forces of Socialism, democracy, and progress . . . On the side of the New World stand the laws of social development, massive revolutionary energy, and the most advanced ideas of the contemporary world . . . One-third of mankind has now taken the road of Socialism . . . and is waging a general offensive against imperialism . . . which was begun in the international arena by the Motherland of October."

For the Soviets, international politics is a means of carrying out a world-historical mission on an unprecedented global scale. For most people in the West, by contrast, "messianism" died long ago — except for the perverted expressions of it in the jingoistic creeds of Mussolini and Hitler, who dreamed of restored Roman Empires and one-thousand-year Reichs. It is sometimes forgotten that present-day Bolshevik mentality is archaic by about 200-400 years, or longer. It is an embalmed thing, like Lenin's *kukl'* (doll) in the Red Square Mausoleum, but it is nevertheless quite life-like. Far from being "progressive," Soviet ideology is the most retrogressive, reactionary creed imaginable.

In the way it conjures up earthly paradises, it is reminiscent of Medieval or Renaissance-spawned utopias, or of the 18th-century French *philosophes* who contrived earthly paradises of the type parodied by Voltaire in *Candide*. As to the Lenin-Stalin-Khrushchev-Brezhnev-*et al.* one-man dictatorship over the proletariat, it has the feel of the absolutism of, say, the "Sun King," Louis XIV, of *"l'etat c'est moi,"* I am the state. The "father of Russian Marxism," George Plekhanov, once compared Bolshevism to an ancient South American Indian, priest-caste dictatorship, while a number of anti-Stalin ex-Communists have seen in the Soviet system a reversion to the divine kingship of Byzantium. Likewise, in the state-controlled, or "nationalized," economy of Soviet Communism, one is reminded of the archaic mercantilist system of the 17th century or of the guilds of the Middle Age, with their political strictures against "free enterprise" and a free market and their state monopoly over industry and commerce. But compared to these outworn Western phenomena, the Soviet centralized management and direction of socio-economic activity in the state are far more sweeping and possess what the Russians call *"razmakh"* (totalitarian breadth), for which there is no clear historical parallel.

Some Westerners — e.g., former Ambassadors George Kennan, Averell Harriman, or Charles W. Yost in their late years — like to imagine that Stalin, Molotov, Gromyko, Brezhnev, Malik, and the rest, despite Marxist-Leninist doctrine, choose to play by the accepted rules of international behavior.

Such people refuse to face the fact that the Soviets not only explicitly reject the old norms as "bourgeois" antiques, they concretely behave in world affairs exactly as their creed says they must: by flouting the rules. This double-standard, two-track, or simply Janus-faced Soviet way of demanding, say, "noninterference" by other states while practicing interference to the hilt themselves, has been called the "diopezza" aspect of Russian behavior in international affairs. By Leninists, it's known as "dialectic."

For example, the Soviets act as if they were enthusiastic supporters of disarmament. But they keep very busy arming themselves and others while insisting that Western States "curb the arms-race." In the Soviet Disarmament Memorandum submitted by Foreign Minister Gromyko to the 31st Session of the U.N. General Assembly in September 1977, the world — if it only bothered to read — had an opportunity to acquaint itself with clearly-stated Soviet *diopezza* on the disarmament issue. For after several passages in the Memorandum about the need to scale down the level of arms, make the world "safe" (just for whom was not spelled out), etc., the text went on boldly to assert that arms limitations are made, you see, "between *states, not* between classes and peoples." The "national-liberation struggles" and "people's wars," waged in Africa are not "local wars (between states) . . . but justifiable revolutionary struggles" or "civil wars" that have nothing whatever to do with disarmament. Soviet-made AK-47 automatic rifles, T-34 tanks, PT-76 amphibious tanks, AT-3 "Sagger" anti-tank missiles, SA-7 "SAM's," 122 mm. mounted rocket-launchers, MIG fighters in several versions, armored personnel carriers, artillery of various descriptions, etc., are today air-or sea-lifted to such places as Mozambique and Angola, Ethiopia and Iraq, Congo-Brazzaville and Libya — the list goes on . . . These arms are used within countries to forcibly effect changes in government, in a Marxist direction, or they are sent to certain countries so that they may wage "liberation struggles" against other, neighboring countries. Intra-/inter-"peoples'" struggles, says Moscow, are not interstate wars. And so, disarmament is irrelevant.

The arms traffic from the USSR to places of revolutionary and/or strategic interest to Moscow has reached such proportions that the Soviet Union now leads the world in arms transfers of conventional weaponry of the type most useful for answering what Brezhnev calls the dictates of the Soviet "revolutionary conscience." (The U.S. used to be the leader in many categories of arms transfers worldwide, largely because the types of arms it sold, to countries purchasing them for self-defense — Iran, for example — were ultra-sophisticated and, thus, expensive, and included such hardware as electronic-sensing equipment, F-15 or F-5E jets, anti-aircraft guns, anti-tank weapons, and so on.) The arms traffic promises to be stepped up by the Soviets, despite a leveling-off of the rate of growth of their economy and despite, of course, any pacifist or fellow-traveler sentiment in other countries that might be shocked by such Soviet behavior.

The "positive" content of peaceful coexistence/detente, then, amounts merely to this, in the Soviet construction: 1) postponement of any major show-down between East and West over the East's subsidization of the spread of Soviet-style Socialism; 2) intimidation of the West, during the postponement, lest any military or civilian leaders there think that the USSR can be out-deterred, in conventional or strategic weapons, by the NATO countries, 3) use of the threat to employ strategic weapons in order to keep revolutionary-supportive actions by the Soviets — in Africa, the Middle East, South or Southeast Asia, and so on — unimpeded and uninterrupted by the "class" or "imperialist" enemy.

In order to implement this three-pronged strategy, the Soviet Union has set about concertedly modernizing its arms so as to increase its ability to intervene in distant places, or "project" its power. This has meant, especially, the development of its air-transport, in the form of the huge Antonov long-range carriers, or of its sea-life capacity, a concomitant of the fact that the Soviet merchant fleet is now the world's largest in terms of freighters and of their "deadweight" (carrying capacity) — respectively, as of the mid-1970's, over 1,700 freighters, 10,500,000 long tons of deadweight.

Piecing together all the elements making up Soviet intentions and behavior throughout the world, we get the following conglomerate:

— the Chosen Nation has a worldwide revolutionary mission, which it fulfills by shipping arms and military advisers to areas in which there are "revolutionary situations";

— conventional arms are being perfected so as to enhance the effectiveness of the mission;

— quoting the first post-Stalin Soviet Premier, Georgi Malenkov, "lessening of tensions (detente) may lead to the disintegration (of the North Atlantic bloc)" — i.e., by sowing the seeds of dulcet-toned detente, "internal strife" and "contradictions" within the Western camp (Malenkov) could be encouraged — when there is no apparent threat against which to prepare, the West's attention flags as to military defense, NATO integrity, etc. Or to quote present-day Soviet leaders, detente abets national-liberation struggles and other revolutionary activity because the accompanying "code of detente establishes rules . . . for relationships between states which will forbid military adventures" by those who attempt to "counteract the revolutionary process" (Brezhnev);

— the present world situation is one of neither peace nor war; or, put another way, the ultimate struggle between Socialism and Capitalism is already underway ("World War III has, in fact, begun"), although the "war" may never reach the ultimate stage of an actual exchange of thermonuclear-tipped rockets and bombs.

Finally, as to the revolutionary uses of that ultimate stage of third world war, the Soviets have been elusive. Imagine, for a moment, if on our side official U.S. government literature said, "We hope that nuclear war does not come. But if it does, we will win it and we will get rid of Communism once and for all." This is exactly what the Soviets are saying, changing, of course, the word "Communism" to "Capitalism." Here it is, from the Soviet book, *Marksizm-Leninizm o Voine i Armii (Marxism-Leninism on War and the Army)*, published in several editions, the latest in the mid-1970's. It's dull reading but try to stick with it:

"The 'fetishism' of armed violence and its isolation from politics (i.e., forgetting that war is but the continuation of politics by other means) has assumed a new 'nuclear' form under contemporary conditions. Some bourgeois ideologists maintain that nuclear missile weaponry, like the sorcerer-apprentice's broomstick, has eliminated political considerations respecting a third world war . . . as though free of any class-political content . . .

"Other bourgeois ideologists, who realize that a thermonuclear war would be fatal to capitalism . . . declare incorrectly that the interrelationship between politics and war (as Clausewitz and Lenin explained) has lost all significance . . .

"The social, class content of nuclear missile war and its aims will be determined by politics . . . (our) side's view of war consists in seeing its lawful and just counteraction to aggression, the natural right and sacred duty of progressive mankind to destroy imperialism, its bitterest enemy, the source of destructive wars . . .

"Armed struggle with the use of nuclear missiles and other weapons will ultimately be subordinated to the interests of a definite policy and will become a means for achieving definite political aims."

Elusively worded, yes, but explicity and between the lines this compounded message is nevertheless imparted:

— don't "fetishize" — that is, exaggerate — the destructiveness of thermonuclear weapons or a third world war;

— the Clausewitz-Lenin formula about war being merely the continuation of politics — in this case, continuation of Marxist-Leninist revolutionary politics — is *just as applicable in the thermonuclear age* as it was in the age of machine-guns and dirigibles (when Lenin developed and modernized the Clausewitzian formula);

— a thermonuclear world war, which "could only be initiated by the other, imperialist side," would surely be "revolutionary" and "just," because it would finally wipe capitalism and imperialism off the face of the earth.

Other Soviet writings, and government officials, have made that last point above quite explicit — to wit, the present chief of the "political commissariat" of the USSR Ministry of Defense, Gen. A. A. Yepishev, has boldly stated:

"A third world war, if imperialism should start one, will be the decisive class conflict between the two antagonistic world systems. From side of the imperialist states, this war will be the continuation of the criminal, reactionary, and aggressive policies of imperialism. But from the side of the Soviet Union and the countries of the Socialist Commonwealth, this war will be the continuation of the revolutionary policies of freedom and independence of the Socialist state, a guarantee of the construction of Socialism and Communism and a legal and justified counteraction to aggression."

The phrase about "if imperialism should start one" — a third world war — would appear to save the otherwise blood-curdling frankness, with which General Yepishev treats the "positive" side of World War III, from an outright endorsement of the apocalyptic, catastrophic way of assuring the complete triumph of Communism. Everything appears to be relatively less sanguinary, in this Soviet statement and the others like it, as long as the Russians say that such a war would be forced upon them by the other side.

Not quite. One or two further explanations are necessary. First, the current political-military line on preventing World War III has itself an ominous ring. It consists in the Soviet claim that the Kremlin can "preclude," "cut off," "preempt," "foreclose," "crush," etc. — all these words derived from their Russian equivalents — the very unleashing of fullfledged *war* by the "imperialists." Two samples of this idea of *preemption* follow:

"The Armed Forces must be capable, under any conditions, of frustrating a surprise attack by the aggressor with the use of either nuclear or conventional weapons, and with rapid, devastating blows, destroying his main missile-nuclear weapons and troop formations" (from Marshal Andrei Grechko's *Na Strazhe Mira i Stroitel'stva Kommunizma* [*Guarding Peace and the Construction of Communism*]).

"Surprise allows one to forestall the enemy in the execution of his strikes, to catch him unawares, to paralyze his will, sharply reduce his combat capability, disorganize his command and control, and create favorable conditions for the destruction of even superior forces" (V. E. Savkin, *Osnovniye Printsipy Operativnovo Iskusstva i Taktiki* [*Fundamental Principles of Military Art and Tactics*]).

In other words, the advantage of striking first — with a preemptive blow (*uprezhdainshchii udar*) — consists in the ability to take the enemy by surprise, thus "frustrating" or "forestalling" his own use of surprise by his launching the first attack.

As Stalin was fond of saying, "Clear, one would think."

All too clear. But does the solution lie in an American "preventive-war" strategy? Anyone who suggested it, back in the Cold War years, was considered a lunatic. Today, the idea is made even more insane by the fact that the weapons have increased so tremendously in their killing power since the 1950's. Today, conservative estimates are that both sides would lose several dozen million people in an exchange of thermonuclear rockets and bombs, whether launched from planes, cruise missiles, MIRVed missiles, or from submarines carrying MIRVed missiles. On the other hand, it is true, the Soviets are better prepared than we to save large numbers of their work force because of the civil-defense training they have given citizens over the years, and because their society is in general "commanded" more than ours. Moreover, the Russians have shown themselves to be callous enough on other occasions when it has come down to realizing their sacred Communist ends, by using any and all means to reach them. Ten million peasants, for example, were sacrificed for the purpose of collectivization.

Perhaps the most chilling thought is that the Russians would not be beneath launching a war — of whatever kind — and blaming its initiation on the other side. Fact is there are several historical precedents for this kind of Soviet pretext-plus-initiation-of-hostilities behavior.

They did it, for example, in the case of the 1939-40 "Winter War" with Finland. In November 1939, they blamed the Finns for their alleged lobbing of artillery shells on Leningrad. But an independent League of Nations investigating commission exposed this explanation as a pretext: The Russians had shelled themselves. The same fabricated pretext was used in Korea in June 1950, and again in Vietnam in the summer of 1964. In both instances, Communist troops crossed in force into foreign territory (across the 38th and 18th Parallels respectively) while blaming the other side for the initiation of war.

In other words, the Soviet record is terrible. "Mutual trust," Brezhnev once said early in the detente honeymoon, is an inseparable ingredient of U.S.-Soviet relations and their improvement. But the Kremlin has never admitted the hoaxes it has perpetrated in the past before it or its friends launched a given war or "struggle." As a result, distrust of Soviet behavior is still very much alive. At the very start of the detente process, in fact, Moscow again indulged itself in blaming the other side for its own, aggressive movement of Communist troops: in the case of the invasion and occupation of Czechoslovakia in August 1968. The pretext on that occasion was the alleged preparation in West Germany of unnamed "forces" whose mission it was to over-throw the established Socialist order in Dubcek-ruled Czechoslovakia, and with Dubcek's own connivance.

Not even Communists in the West have yet gotten over this ruse, by which a "fraternal country" was invaded and its government forcibly altered so as to suit Moscow's purposes. Czechoslovakia, together with the December 1979 Soviet invasion of Afghanistan, remains as a warning to those who still entertain the comfortable thought that the Russians have somehow changed in the thermonuclear era into trustworthy guardians of "bourgeois" rules of international behavior for the avoidance of military conflict, and the violation of other nations' borders.

"The sovereignty of individual Socialist countries," said *Pravda* on September 26, 1968, "cannot be juxtaposed to the interests of world Socialism and the world revolutionary movement."

If the sovereignty of "Socialist countries" is themselves up for grabs, what about the sovereignty of capitalist, semi-capitalist, or social-democratic countries? Obviously, theirs is even less secure.

Chapter 16

Myth of Isolationism

"Once the decision is made to use military power to settle a
political issue, that power should be used to its full effectiveness to get the war over with as quickly as possible. All
other considerations should be secondary. *That* is the way
to reduce *civilian and military casualties*.

Adm. U.S. Grant Sharp

The verb, "to isolate," comes from the same root
as "insular," or island-like. "No man's an island," runs the
phrase by John Donne — nor is a country. Nor is the United
States of America, which indeed, looks like an island surrounded
by the Atlantic and Pacific Oceans.

In days of yore, going back to Washington and Jefferson, it surely appeared that America was and always would be
an island. Of course, those were the days of horse-and-buggy. It
was also the time of clippership transportation. Recall that it took
so long to get across the Atlantic by ship that the War of 1812 was
still blazing on, with people getting killed, although the peace
treaty ending the war had already been signed in Ghent, Belgium,
weeks earlier. Unfortunately, news, unlike light, did not travel in
those days at 186,000 miles/sec. as it does in these days of radio,
T.V., and Intertel Satellite. General Stonewall Jackson's men

must have been as dismayed, as they were glad, to learn that the war had "ended" some two weeks before (on Christmas Eve, 1814). But 2,000 troops of the British forces and almost 100 Americans had become fatalities of post-truce combat that lasted until the news of the treaty reached our shores in January 1815.

So, obviously, the world is much "smaller" today than it was 200 years ago. Too, time — meaning news and historical information — passes more quickly than before so that the historical reels of information accumulate "film" with amazing rapidity. Result: History is "made" quicker as more and more countries get drawn into the world-historical process. This involvement affects our own country more than any other because we are the world's most powerful and "involved" country, producing almost half of the entire world's Gross National Product. And yet, America remains the home of a most pernicious myth — harmful, not only because it is false and misleading but because it is dangerous to the country's security and self-respect.

Nowhere has the effect of American *neo-isolationism* been more telling in recent times than in the case of the Vietnam War.

The war in Vietnam was called a "T.V. war." Apparently, it only lightly touched and faintly horrified Americans, as they viewed fragments of it on their sets. Still, the war made a mighty impact. If nothing else, it reminded many people — most of whom directly knew of no one engaged in actual combat in Southeast Asia — of where and how "their" $130 billion was spent. For these people, and they were right, the money went down the drain. Logically, many asked, "Why did we get involved in the mess in the first place?" Only a small minority wondered, as some do belatedly today, "When we got into it, why didn't we go all the way and insure victory over the aggressors from the North?" Nothing wins like victory, nothing loses like defeat, runs the folk adage.

Everyone knows the answer to above question: We fought the war with one arm tied behind our backs. But why did we wing ourselves this way? One reason was that we were afraid: The Chinese might come in, or, God forbid, the well-armed Russians, with planes, tanks, troops, missiles. Perhaps the more important reason was the thought that we had done enough damage already, it was time to stop. (These perceptions come through in *The Pentagon Papers*.)

While we worried and agonized, the North Vietnamese and the Vietcong, with advice and materiel forthcoming from the Russians, and to a lesser extent from the Chinese,

worked doggedly to keep us hemmed in, boxed in, squeezed —
the Soviets actually employ a word for this, of which they are
rightfully proud, "*potesnit*'" — i.e., locked into that semi-
paralyzed, one-arm-behind-our-backs state. A cartoon published
in *Pravda* illustrated *potesnit*' — a giant, America, bound to the
ground with stakes while Lilliputians scampered about as they
bound the ropes tighter. In effect, we had allowed ourselves to be
hemmed in by accepting depictions of the war — myths can
create perceptions better than "reality" can — in the form of a
political morality play, instead of the heartless clashing of arms
that any war really is. We would do our level best. But: We would
surely not bomb ARVN's water-supply aqueducts. We would do
our level best. But: We would not attempt to interdict supplies
flowing to ARVN from China and Russia to the north, by land or
by sea. We would bomb the hell out of 'em. But: We would not
care all that much about accuracy, being satisfied if we scared
them "to their senses." Most of this shilly-shallying is broadcast
clearly in *The Pentagon Papers*, that purloined drivel, which, in
any case, constituted only a small share of the inside memoranda,
interpretations, and conversations about the war and how it could
better be fought by our side.

As another cliché runs, war is like pregnancy,
half-way is impossible. By failing to prosecute the war to the hilt,
we decided to play safe and play fair and fight a ¼-war. So, not
surprisingly, we lost it. The other side, of course, fought the war
on its own terms, and made peace — and broke it — also on its
own terms. By the time Nixon and Kissinger had surveyed the
ongoing Vietnam debacle, and the fast-growing Senate disaffec-
tion in 1969-70, which was rising to the 50% mark (crossing this line
in both houses would have meant scissoring the funds for the
Administration's war effort), they began to behave as if they were
aware, at least, that they might be out-foxed by the enemy: The
Communists made peace overtures, yes, but we had to make sure
that they did not take undue advantage of any lull in the fighting.
Which the Communists proceeded to do, of course, beginning in
March 1972, when they struck in force, using all-out
conventional-war tactics, against the South.

Nixon's and Kissinger's response was: 1) laser pin-
point bombing — that devastatingly accurate way of hitting the
enemy where it really hurt (e.g., bridges over which his troops
and materiel flowed, no matter where the routes might be; 2)
mining of the North's harbors, including the main one of
Haiphong, so that no more Red-flag and other cargo ships could

enter or leave port and preventing any more of the lethal cargoes in those bottoms from reaching the Cong or ARVN troops.

Some people in the know have since estimated that had we continued with both of these effective measures — or, better, if we had only started them years sooner — we would have won the war. This is no mere Monday-morning-quarterbacking.

In Michael Charlton's and Anthony Moncrieff's revealing post-Vietnam book, *Many Reasons Why The American Involvement in Vietnam,* the authors point out how American laser-beam bombing of Hanoi, in December 1972, "overwhelmed [the city's] defenses . . . Industrial capacity in North Vietnam was virtually brought to a halt." It was this bombing that forced the North Vietnamese and their VC toadies (remember all that baloney, during the war, about Vietcong independence, postwar "coalition government," etc.?) seriously to talk peace, instead of stalling over the precise seating arrangements, the shape of the negotiating table, and so on. Unfortunately, however, the U.S. chose not to exploit its military advantage at this important stage of the game. For us, it was already "too late," in the sense that the country seemed hide-bound to pull out of Southeast Asia, no matter what. Writing in the Charlton-Moncrieff book, Warren Nutter, Assistant Secretary of Defense under Nixon, argues that if we had done laser and/or saturation bombing "on the order of what was done in World War II . . . the war could have been ended very quickly at any time." Mere tonnage of bombs, which in Vietnam amounted to more than was dropped by us in World War II, was not the point; targets north of the DMZ, saturation, and accuracy were what was crucial.

Obviously, we didn't bomb this way. Nor did we do many other things that would have won the war. Had we done them, we could have made the point about American resolve to oppose aggression in an era when too many Western countries are willing to do precious little to stem the Communist red tide. Our lack of resolve is today's topic of conversation, say, in Saudi Arabia, where oil-rich Arabs wonder out loud if America has the strength of will to assert itself and defend its most obvious interests, along with those of the whole West, whether these interests extend all the way to the geostrategic Persian Gulf, to the Horn or to the northwestern segment of the Indian Ocean. Iran, in taking and keeping our hostages at the U.S. Embassy in Teheran, was obviously emboldened by the "post-Vietnam" American syndrome of slack resolve.

Vietnam remains a bone stuck in our throats. We

declined, until it was too late, to mine the ARVN harbors and to develop lasers; as to Marine landings on the North's beaches — operations we had done so effectively in the Korean War in 1951-2 — we never mounted a single one. We lost a golden opportunity in the early 1970's to retrieve what had been lost since 1965 because of morality-play tactics. As someone has said, the Vietnam War was not lost by our side in the rice paddies of Southeast Asia but amid the misty wistfulness of Foggy Bottom.

And the myth of defeatism was encouraged in other quarters.

During the war, you could hear, as I did, one of those handsome, oval-toned "newsmen" on T.V. reading that it was "hard for Americans to imagine" that their country's interests stretched "several thousand miles overseas, measuring the distance from Washington, D.C., to the battlefields of Vietnam." But since when is the Malacca Strait any less strategic — as the waterway through which pass the Japanese tankers with their precious cargoes of oil bound for that country's industry and which is also used by our own Sixth Fleet — because it is several thousand miles away? Suez, the Strait of Hormuz, the Indian Ocean, our sources of oil, are even thousands of more miles away: Does that make these areas any less important to us?

Is it not clear that American *perceptions* of the war in Southeast Asia led to our losing it? One wonders if the perceptions arose "spontaneously" and "automatically." Again, aren't myths or perceptions like dirty stories? No one in particular seems to invent them but they surely do acquire enormous virulence by the way and the extent to which they are propagated.

As for Dezinformatsiya — that branch of the KGB engaged in spreading misinformation — it was busy, both with spinning and spreading the various spider-web myths with which to ensnare American flies. Too, they were helped by certain disenchanted (or worse) Americans, some of them in editorial positions, and for whom the war in Vietnam became an obsessive hatred utterly blinding their reason and common sense. It still does. Remember these widely-disseminated, Dezinformatisya gems? You still encounter them:

— America was perpetrating "crimes" in Vietnam, scene of the "dirty war," Lt. Calley being only one of the lesser perpetrators while the main villain was the "military-industrial complex" — indeed, a whole "monopoly-capitalist" institution, no less; "Communist massacres at Hue," — where's that again??;

— the longer we upset the Soviets by continuing our "intervention" in Vietnam, the longer we would have to wait in order to reach agreement with them on scaling down the arms race — cleverly, Brezhnev & Co. timed their hints about "detente," a summit, and SALT precisely when American resolve to prosecute a truly man-size war began to show wear around the edges. Foreign Minister Andrei Gromyko, the notorious *khitrets* (trickster) with a number of lies to his credit already (e.g., denial of Soviet implanting of missiles on Cuba in 1962), lofted his first detente balloon in 1968, appropriately at Turtle Bay, in the U.N. General Assembly;

— Vietnam protesters, if not the Vietcong itself, should be depicted as heroes of our time deserving our respect (many of our young, home-grown protesters, despite or because of their unmitigated hatred and passion, were clearly confused, and perhaps in many cases understandably so, since the losing side of a dispute is hardly worth the joining or laying down your life, if it came to that); the *heroism of dissent* was far more appealing;

— this war, any war, only lines the pockets of "war profiteers," the "armaments-makers," or, that is, civilian members of the notorious "military-industrial complex," who "instigated" and "continued" the war (See Chapter 13, on "MIC").

I am not suggesting that the KGB invented the anti-Vietnam War protest movement — although it certainly gave it assistance. At very least, it was Soviet policy to direct its overseas propaganda and disinformation effort, and the funds, in the ways indicated above (I collected piles of this literature finding that much of it, to judge by type-faces and recurring, tell-tale misspellings, had been run off on the same presses, whether in New York or London). The propaganda — of KGB orgin within Dezinformatsiya, according to ex-KGBists, who ought to know — was made to dovetail and lend support to those confused Americans of pacifist persuasion, or to those who toyed with "capitulationist" sentiments (the Soviets invented the term, capitulationist, and are well aware of its subversive potency during an unpopular war or in a revolutionary situation in which the "bourgeois" powers-that-be must "capitulate"). Above all, the familiar myth-picture came into focus: the mythic depiction of the war in Vietnam as a political morality play with American villains opposing the sandaled, Oriental defenders of social justice; a picture-sub.titute for the brutal reality of military conflict which had to be, one would have thought, waged on strictly military terms.

On numerous occasions, most of us saw those red, blue and yellow Vietcong colors neatly painted by vandals on U.S. Post Office mailboxes; the U.S. Post Office, you see, is at least in the same branch of the same government that includes the Pentagon. When I saw them in New York, I often wondered to myself, Who made those beautiful templates? Who supplied the paint and commissioned the daubers? And what about the films produced in North Vietnam and rolled at the "Hippie Church" in Greenwich Village, amid well-drilled, cheering throngs in the audience? Who supplied this celluloid, rented the space, recruited the claques?

I had the unique opportunity, when the war was at its agonizing worst (in the late 1960's), to attend a well-heeled, "radical-chic" cocktail party on the Upper East Side of Manhattan. Everyone has *that* cocktail party which he or she will never forget; this one was certainly "it." I will have to omit the names of the hosts as well as those of the many famous people who attended it, including a well-known playwright with whom I had a most intense conversation.

After he had declaimed on the evil intents of American intervention in Vietnam, Mr. X proceeded to enlighten me on the aims and techniques of the New Left in our country. He and many others, he said, made large contributions to this "cause"; he wanted to clarify for me, he said, how the "leadership" and the contributors regarded the left's mission.

"The worse everything gets," he said, "the better it is for the Cause." He went on to explain that the more "aggravation" caused by continuation of the Vietnam War the better: Anger and frustration only prepare the soil all that more for socialist-type remedies of the "overall capitalist situation." "Until the country sees that the socialist way — state ownership and management of property and the means of production, state planning, and so on — is the only way, it will be necessary for us to 'remind the public' of the dire straits in which the country will remain — until it adopts socialism."

Upon hearing this, I was immediately reminded of the revolutionary philosophy of the nineteenth-century Russian Narodniks, upon which I happened to have done the better part of the work on my Doctorate a few years previous. A Russian Narodnik radical of the 1870's, Peter Tkachev, had boldly stated, "Progress [i.e., improvement of social and economic conditions under the Old Order] strengthens enslavement that much more, sharpens the weapons of oppression, and complicates the struggle against the ruling classes.'' So thought Tkachev, the ''forerunner of Lenin,'' as he is known. Worsening conditions — and doing everything possible to help them worsen — *abet* the Cause, the will to struggle, etc. Paul Axelrod, the Russian Marxist who became disillusioned with Lenin, once described this Tkachevist-Leninist notion of ''worse-is-better'' as a basically misanthropic idea, a harmful myth, used merely to oil the mechanism of Bolshevik-style revolutionary organizations. ''A philosophy of progress,'' Tkachev kept insisting, ''is harmful to the success of the revolutionary cause . . . It is a philosophy of compromise . . . and of delay.'' Remarks such as these, which were encountered by Lenin when he thoroughly read and ingested the ideas of Tkachev, are reflected in a number of Lenin's own writings (e.g., the 1903 work, *What Is To Be Done?*)

These thoughts entered my mind as Mr. X continued his diatribe on the tactics and strategy of the New Left. Since then, I have pondered his, and others', words about worse-is-better. Could this rationale be extended to other stances taken by New Left types today? Say, opposing the construction of nuclear-energy facilities in the U.S.? Granted that there are risks in going nuclear, but the risks are as great or greater with hydroelectric, and surely with coal-driven generators, according to a number of energy specialists. The radioactive leaks at the Three Mile Island plant near Harrisburg in the spring of 1979 was a freakish accident. It was, in fact, the only serious mishap, in terms of a threat of radioactive pollution to numbers of people, to occur among all 72 nuclear reactors operating in the country — in Pennsylvania, New York, New Jersey, South Carolina, Arkansas, Florida, California, and other states. As to New Left, *et al.*, endorsement and support of radical environmentalism: This only helps frustrate, of course, our switching to coal as an alternative to oil, almost half of which must be imported from the tension-ridden Middle East and one of the targets for Soviet influence. New Left sponsorship of the allegedly safe and ''feasible'' alternative, solar energy, appears at times to be more ruse than a sincere or positive suggestion. Going solar is prohibitively expensive and, according to independent researchers with no axe to grind, simply unrealistic as a viable substitute for either oil or coal.

Sometimes you get the uncomfortable feeling that the radicals, the environmentalists, the ban-the-nukes crowd, and the anti-Pentagon propagandists are all of one piece: They are committed to causes that are distinctly detrimental to *national security*.

From another angle, they play upon the isolationistic instincts, if that is what they are, of the American people. Or they exploit other popular misconceptions, such as the notion that America is potentially self-sufficient.

Once, late in 1979, I appeared on the New York TV interview program, "Straight Talk." Joining me were two quasi-New Left types, who, among other things, insisted that America was economically self-sufficient, or that it surely could totally be if it only tried. Russia, on the other hand, they maintained, was not autarchic and relied "solidly" on East-West trade. The point they were attempting to drive home was that America is cavalier in its foreign-trade, multi-national corporate business, etc.; all this is expendable to us, a mere luxury. The USSR, on the other hand, has a deep, vested interest in healthy international commerce — and the peace that is supposedly encouraged by such business-as-usual. Of course, I had to point out to them that the exact reverse was the case: Our country is strongly dependent upon the rest of the world, and not only for oil, but also for a host of other critical raw materials used in manufacture. On the other hand, the Soviet Union is vastly more economically independent than we; for it, East-West trade is largely expendable (except, perhaps, for grain and a few items of high technology, which, in any case, may be obtained from other countries besides the U.S.). Bottom line: Our neo-isolationism clashes violently with our dependence on the rest of the world, and that is particularly true in the energy (oil) field. Soviet "dependence," by contrast, is confined to a few commodities and the one raw material of grain; for this and other reasons, her go-it-alone policy has worked rather well. She can even endure playing the role of an isolated, post-Afghanistan pariah, if necessary; she is not afraid of ostracism by the "world community."

Vietnam was the bastard-child of the myth of American neo-isolationism. It is linked to another blind spot in the American psyche: ignorance of geopolitics. This discipline, and guide to a superpower's foreign policy, was once described by one of its founding-fathers, Halford J. Mackinder, as seeing the "political interconnection of things on the surface of the globe." About geopolitics, as useful myth and guide to action, see the next chapter.

ABOUT OTHERS . . .

Chapter 17

Myth of Geopolitics

"The road to Paris and London lies via the towns of Afghanistan . . ."

Leon Trotsky

"Under conditions of the changed correlation of forces — in decisive measure due to the increased power of Socialism — the anti-imperialist forces now have acquired the ability to impose upon imperialism such principles of international relations that are consistent with the interests of peace and of Social Progress."

Kommunist, Moscow

Nineteen seventy-nine marked the 60th anniversary of the publication, in February 1919, of the theories and global perceptions of British geographer Halford J. Mackinder (1861-1947) developed in his book, *Democratic Ideals and Reality.* These perceptions are alive and well today. Indeed, the present-day strategies of the military superpowers, the U.S., Soviet Union, and China, bear tell-tale traces of Mackinder's assumptions. In particular, the USSR, an early "student" of geopolitics, has all too obviously based its currently aggressive foreign policy and thrusting into strategic regions of the world upon the totalist, global perspective. Soviet doctrine has asserted since 1965: The time has come to "take the global offensive against the positions of imperialism." The United States, once a pioneer in geopolitics (e.g., the bullish 1890's with its "Manifest Destiny" and its Mahanist navalism), is also in the process of redesigning and redirecting its political and military strategy along lines of Mahan-Mackinder and the glosses made upon the globalist-geostrategic doctrine by Nicholas Spykman and others. The third power, the People's Republic of China, has also — belatedly — taken up the pursuit of geopolitics. The current PRC slogan of "modernization" embodies geopolitical perceptions and premises for eventually extending Chinese influence, perhaps mainly defensively in the beginning, beyond the discrete borders of the Middle Kingdom. Deputy Premier Teng Hsiao-ping made this revision of traditional Chinese insularism quite clear, among other places, in his interview with *Time* Magazine during his visit to the U.S. in 1979.

"The Soviet strategy in Asia is to put down a strategic cordon around the continent, stretching from the Mediterranean, the Red Sea, the Indian Ocean and up to Haishenwei (Vladivostok), and using the 'Cuba of Asia,' Vietnam, as its hatchetman." This Chinese assessment of the Afro-Asian nexus in Soviet strategic thinking is matched by similar perceptions in the West. "The Soviet Union," write two American military-strategy specialists, "has staged a break-out from its land-locked position . . . that has enabled Moscow to threaten, compromise, and in some cases supplant key points of U.S. forward deployments in Europe and Asia." Australian Prime Minister Malcolm Fraser has asserted that the Soviet presence in the Near and Far East is a "manifestation of its global power, its capacity to reach out into any part of the world and act in a destabilizing manner." "The Persian Gulf, the Indian Subcontinent, and both continental and maritime Southeast Asia," writes an Australian scholar, are all links in a "global, multilevel power game" for influence in an area which is not only an arena for the ongoing Sino-Soviet struggle but one that is rich in raw materials (oil, copper, zinc, *et al.*) and which contains the key countries of the Third World.

Such statements reflect a new consciousness on the part of astute observers of the world scene. They sense the "to-talistic," global look to the most significant events occurring in recent years affecting relations between the world's greatest military powers as well as a host of medium- and small-size nation-states. Above all, the emerging pattern of Soviet expansionism that is tied to an offensive geostrategy is awakening the world to the eternal truths, or myths of geopolitics.

In its essence, geopolitics, and the strategies based upon it, is a working hypothesis, a scheme for perceiving the world, a species of Kantian "regulative idea." It perceives, or "manipulates," the world in a certain way; it is one of several possible techniques for "worldmaking," to use Nelson Goodman's term. Like Riemann's non-Euclidean geometry, the projections by Mackinder and his students amount to constructs of the permanent physical realities but also of dynamic political factors of the globe. At the same time, the projections depend on the projector's premises and goals. But some realistic, "permanent" imperatives about the globe press down on the strategist. He must ponder the locations of countries; the landmass or maritime characteristics or orientation of certain regions (in which tradition, too, acts almost like a permanent factor); key natural resources and their accessibility; permanent, geographical relationships existing between whole continents, regions, and nation-states, relationships that also reflect traditional attitudes; and fighting ability and tradition. All these "moments" will determine the makeup of the formulas of geopolitics regulating and underwriting strategies, political and military, especially for the most powerful states, for whom global reach is feasible, even necessary.

Combining Mackinder's insights with those of his foremost successors — e.g., Hans Speir, Spykman, Colin S. Gray, W. Scott Thompson, *et al.* — you get the following *axioms of modern geopolitics:*

- Eurasia and Africa together constitute a World-Island which, if it were ever controlled or dominated by a single large nation-state, would guarantee to that state the advantage of domination over the rest of the world; the geographic base of such a likely dominator, or "hegemonist," is the Heartland of Russia, the centrally- and crucially-located country at the "pivotal point" of the World-Island.
- The land, sea, and countries that lie adjacent to the World-Island, and which are uncommonly rich in natural resources, constitute the Rimlands, "crescents," or marginal littoral, seas, or islands whose geographic importance becomes enormous because: a) a power with preponderant influence over them may deny access to any challenger of the World-Island hegemonist; b) the Rimlands may serve as a springboard for the World-

Island, Heartland-power's ability to "box in" or "hem in" (in Russian, "potesnit") and eventually dominate the Insular nation-states of the British Isles, the United States, Japan, Australia, New Zealand, *et al.*, that lie scattered beyond the central core, or base, of Eurasia.

In my view, it is, in fact, about time that the general public, not to mention halls of academia in the U.S., became acquainted (really, reacquainted) with what Mackinder called the "political interconnection of things on the surface of the globe." For too long, scholars and policymakers in the democracies have thought in ad hoc, partial, or "theater-oriented" terms about actual or potential conflicts and wars. An orbiting cosmonaut or astronaut has seen the world more realistically — and totally — than a number of experts down below. Mackinder, Spykman, Gray, and others have directed their efforts mainly at achieving a recasting of the Western mind so that it may perceive the larger pattern. As a Russian admiral wrote in 1899 in his published appreciation of the writings on navalist geopolitics by U.S. Navy Rear Admiral Alfred Thayer Mahan (1840-1914): "localized strategies only lead to missing the forest for the trees."

It is noteworthy that at least two suitable candidates for the role of dominator over the Heartland and, consequently, over the Eurasian World-Island, did *not* permit themselves to develop cretinized, partial political-military strategies. They opted instead for totalistic projections.

With its self-styled master of geopolitics, Herr Doktor Karl Haushofer (1860-1946), Nazi Germany conceived itself to be the authentic occupier of the Heartland. Germany's invasion of Russia in 1941, after it had already occupied the western extension of Eurasia, or west Eurasian "peninsula" (minus, significantly, England), was an effort to reach a geostrategic "final solution" of the geopolitical equation first outlined by Mackinder and glossed by Haushofer. Germany's failure to capture the Heartland was not only the result of military and political blunders. It stemmed from an essential weakness in much of Haushofer's basic conceptualization, his premises, projections; he was, in effect, a poor student of Mackinderism. Above all, he forgot that a tenant of true Heartland must be almost entirely self-sufficient, not dependent upon untrustworthy internal/external "colonies."

On the other hand, Russia — under the tsars and commissars — has always been considered the logical base for domination over Eurasia. Long before Mackinder's theses about the Russian Heartland and their echo in Russian strategy, a number of 18th- and 19th-century Western writers, most with no military-strategic background, displayed a keen awareness of the Russian potential for Eurasian domination. In *Encounter* (February 1979), Theodore Draper canvassed the writings of Leibniz in the 18th and Tocqueville and de Pradt in the 19th century and assessed the evidence for an awareness of "Russian supremacism" in their writings. De Pradt, once a chaplain in the French army and a favorite of Napoleon, spoke of Russia as potentially the "dominant power on the continent" of Europe, a state which might not have to actually employ military power but whose threatening presence and "immense power" would result in a "kind of virtual supremacy." (De Pradt thus anticipated the Soviet policy of "Finlandization.")

Likewise, Russians themselves have been conscious of their country's geopolitical advantages and potentialities, as well as of its weaknesses, if it were to play a dominant role in Eurasia. Mahan's writings on geopolitics became the subject of deep study in Russia, both before and after the Bolshevik coup d'état of November 1917. One can find enthusiastic endorsements of Mahan's navalism in the pages of the tsarist *Morskoi Sbornik* (Naval Proceedings) as well as non-attributed borrowings from both Mahan and Mackinder in the postrevolutionary *Morskoi Sbornik* into the Brezhnev period. The Nazi Haushofer was a favorite author of Josef Stalin's. In the 1930's, right up to the Soviet entry into World War II, the Soviet dictator received translations of Dr. Haushofer's writings on geopolitics, which reached Moscow from the Munich-based Institut für Geopolitik. Today the books and articles written by Soviet Admiral S. G. Gorshkov, and his collaborators in both military and civilian circles, are intensely geopolitcal.

At the center of the Soviet strategy for waging the "offensive against imperialism" is the "hemming-in" tactic, or the political-military, geopolitical policy of active denial. The target of this enterprise is the oil-rich Middle East. Denial need not necessarily mean outright seizure or destruction of oil wells. Their nationalization by governments friendly to the Communist Bloc is, of course, helpful; so is nationalization by the governments of "nonaligned" oil-producing countries. Before assaying the Soviet effort with respect to the "capitalist-rear" resource of oil, it is necessary to do what the Soviets themselves have done: Ponder the means by which you might gain an approach to the oil-rich region, above all, near the Persian Gulf, and prepare the process of interrupting the flow of oil by encircling or penetrating the countries from which the oil originates. Ponder, also, the "ultimate" scenario of military engagement — when the gradual process of sapping the imperialist, Near Eastern "rear" might have to be replaced by outright military action, in the form of ground, sea, and air operations.

A Soviet book (*The Developing Countries Work for Peace*, Moscow, 1972, pp. 79-80) asserts that the "Indian Ocean area is increasingly becoming a strategic center . . . as an emergency exit [sic] to Southeast Asia and as a strategic key opening the way to India, East Africa and to a considerable part of the oil-rich Middle East." Perhaps the Soviet appreciation of the strategic importance of this large basin accounts for the fact that the USSR now, (as of 1979-80) leads the world in arms transfers (sales) of military weapons to the LDCs (Less Developed Countries) in the "revolutionary" categories of fighter and bomber aircraft, tanks, anti-aircraft, and artillery weaponry. In the small-arms category, the Soviet-made (actually, Czechoslovak-made) AK-47 automatic rifle, with its banana-shaped cartridge, is by far the most popular gun for establishing a Soviet-backed presence East of Suez. (Such weapons were handed out by the cartons in revolutionary Iran in 1978-9, with Western reports that truckloads of weapons have been crossing the porous border separating the new Islamic state from the Soviet Union to the north.)

"In some situations," writes a Soviet strategist, V. M. Kulish, in his 1972 book, *Military Force and International Relations* (p. 103), "the *knowledge itself* of the Soviet military presence in a given area in which a conflict may be developing *can serve to restrain the imperialists* (and) to prevent them from causing violence against the local population, and to eliminate the threat to the overall peace and international security. It is precisely this type of role that is played by ships of the Soviet Navy in the Mediterranean Sea." Admiral Gorshkov, too, has described the navy's function, in peacetime, of extending Soviet support to "national-liberation forces" far from Soviet shores. Military writers also stress the importance of "cutting off," "pinching," or "hemming in" the "imperialists" so that they are unable to "roll back the inevitable course of history" which leads to "real Socialism." Detente should not act as a deterrent to the various forms of aid given the USSR to Communist or quasi-Communist operations, especially those in the strategic area we have been discussing, a fact that Brezhnev made clear at the 1976 25th Party Congress. ("Detente," he said, "can never mean the freezing of the status quo" worldwide. Likewise, in UN discussions on disarmanent, the Soviets and their immediate allies rule out the inclusion of weapons used in "national-liberation" or Socialist struggle on a list of weapons that are to be objects of disarmament — the Soviet memorandum vis-a-vis UN discussion of this matter, September 1977, made this explicit.) Soviet naval and air blockade of the Eurasian-African Rimlands was demonstrated "almost arrogantly in the worldwide naval exercise held in 1975 — 'Okean-75' . . . Base facilities on the Indian and Atlantic Oceans (means that) the Soviet Union will be well placed to interdict (i.e. deny passage along) the oil-supply route from the Gulf," writes Colin S. Gray. "Should the Russians succeed in incorporating the Middle East into their sphere of influence," writes an American intelligence expert, "the balance of power in the world would be seriously upset."

The "upset" seems well underway: Angola, Ethiopia, South Yemen, Iran, Afghanistan, and Soviet-backed "fronts" throughout the Afro-Eurasian southern perimeter . . . The 1979 Havana conference of "nonaligned nations" was one more milestone marking this expansionist Soviet program for a position of strength in the Third World.

According to the U.S. Committee on Defense Production, the United States will import about 55% of its oil by 1985 from the Middle East. Already Japan must import some 90% of its oil requirements from the Arabian Peninsula-Horn-Persian Gulf area, and that country's raw materials needs are expected to increase in the years ahead by 300% (Of course, other countries in turn depend on Japan as consumers of its products — especially, Indonesia and Australia.) On any single day, upwards to 70 ocean-going merchant ships, most of whom are laden with oil, pass through the Strait of Hormuz, the "choke point" for passage into and out of the Persian Gulf. Most of the Third World borders on the seas and "bays" located in the broad arc reaching from the northwestern sector of the Indian Ocean eastward to Southeast Asia and northwards along the Chinese littoral of the Western Pacific. For these reasons, a Western presence along this line of communication between east and west, and between the "Insular" Western democracies of Britain and the U.S. and the Middle East, is an obvious necessity.

Seventy percent of the earth's surface is covered by water while 95% of its goods are conveyed by sea. This sea-going trade is much more important to the Western democracies than to the USSR and members of its Bloc; should it be interdicted or "denied" in some way, the exports from the Third World could be "hostaged" by the dominant power. Around the "Afro-Asian Ocean" (a way of describing the Indian Ocean), dwell 46% of

Africa's and 47% of the Asian populations. Indeed, it might be argued that there is only one great World Ocean composed of three major "basins": The Pacific, Atlantic, and Indian Oceans, which together dominate two-thirds of the world's surface.

As any schoolboy knows, Great Britain established itself as the dominant ocean-prowling and mercantile power over 200 years ago (400 years ago if the origin is dated back to Elizabeth I). But for a whole spectrum of reasons — some of them "objective," others "subjective" (pertaining to parties and leaders) — Britain had made its withdrawal East of Suez by the late 1960's. This retreat can only be described as one of *the most world-historical developments throughout the whole post-World War II period.* For it left a gaping vacuum in an area that Admiral Mahan once described as encouraging a "gathering of eagles around a central interest." It was no longer a British-dominated, "closed sea" area.

In the late 1960's the only other power that could have assumed the British role in the Afro-Asian Ocean basin was the United States. Our post-World War II strategy, however, did not place much emphasis upon naval mobility, "showing the flag," acquiring anchorages and port facilities in distant places, and so on. Instead, America relied on its well-known technological proficiency, expressed among other ways by the buildup of our strategic air and missile systems. One of the constituent assumptions of MAD (Mutual Assured Destruction) was that the mutual strategic-weapons deterrents — shared between the U.S. and the Soviet Union — were sufficient to deter inter-bipolar war. As to the local-war danger, which was grimly manifest in the case of the Korean and Vietnam Wars, American military strategy appeared to be wedded to the notion or, myth, of "theater-of-operations," or localized warfare, brought to bear to extinguish "brush wars," "national-liberation"-type Communist-inspired combat, etc. At the same time, the location and movements of our world's fleets were designed chiefly to defend the perimeters of American interest — typified by the Japanese-Phillippines arc of defense or the North Atlantic defense perimeter shared with NATO. As the military analysts Alvin Cottrell and Walter Hahn express it, "A bureaucratic planner in Washington may well separate the Indian Ocean from the Pacific Ocean in terms of foreign policy or 'theater of operations' (especially if he himself has been given a delineated purview for one region or the other). Little thought, apparently, was given in Washington (one must assume among the civilians) to the notion of the Afro-Asian Ocean as a "pivot for American naval power in the Pacific on the one hand . . . and for the Sixth and Atlantic fleets on the other." To many on our side, until recently, "U.S. policy toward the Indian Ocean (including the Persian Gulf) was, with some exceptions . . . , one of restraint and constrained military presence. This was in recognition of the fact [?] that the U.S. has no vital interests at stake in the region and that U.S. security interests there are comparatively limited." So stipulated the *U.S. Department of State Bulletin* in 1971.

"What the Soviet Union needs in terms of military preparedness is different from what we need," President Nixon said in 1970. "They're a land power, primarily, with a great potential enemy to the east." Indeed, Russia is a land power, occupying one-sixth of the globe's land surface, with nearly three times the area of the United States. It duly maintains a large army to protect that huge land mass, east and west. But its former, Stalinite military strategy, aimed chiefly at offensive and defensive land war, has lately been augmented by a strategy aimed at fighting and winning both on land and at sea. And long before an actual war begins on land, Russian strategy aims at securing a strong presence at sea, up to and including exportation of Soviet-style Communism and, in time of war, interdicting Afro-Asian lines of communication and defense, not to mention other sectors of the World Ocean. The misleading Nixonian myth took no account of this, obviously.

Since the time of Tsar Peter the Great (1762-1796), Russia has had what Admiral Mahan called a "natural urge" to expand southwards in what Molotov termed 170 years later, "in the direction of the Persian Gulf." (Peter I is said to have left a political testament in which he boldly outlined Russian expansionism; the Soviets deny that he left a testament.) In one of his last writings before he died in 1947, Halford J. Mackinder predicted that Russia, the "new Tenant" (after Nazi Germany's ill-fated sojourn) of the Eurasian Heartland, inevitably would attempt to break out of its alleged land-locked predicament, that Russia sought geographical egress despite Arctic ice or adversary-held choke points at places of exit. For Russia, the World Ocean, and particularly that part of it known as the Afro-Asian (Indian) Ocean, constitutes an irresistible attraction. Coupled to what Mahan called the Russian "tendency necessarily [to] advance," is the existence of a partial vacuum along the Southeast Asian-South Asian-Persian Gulf perimeter. Along this broad arc lie riparian lands containing 931.8 million people, which have in many cases unstable regimes. These states front upon the Indian Ocean with its 28.4 million square miles and its span from

Capetown, South Africa, to Tasmania of 130 degrees of longitude, or 6,500 miles.

In a television interview on October 30, 1978, National Security Adviser Zbigniew Brzezinski remarked that the USSR currently displays a behavior that is based on a myth of "manifest destiny" suggestive of America in the 1890's. The Soviets, he said, feel that they are "on the upswing . . . an upward cycle" in their assertion of power throughout the world. A third of the world's population live under "Marxist" or "Leninist" systems; the number of nation-states of what Moscow calls countries with a "Socialist orientation" keeps increasing — the number now stands at about 20. The leader of the strongest of these states, Leonid Brezhnev, has declared that the time of the global victory of Communism is "approaching."

In conclusion, several options for continued Soviet or Soviet-backed thrusts of various types suggest themselves for the nearest future:

1 Efforts to acquire additional air and sea bases about or within the perimeter for the "paramount" state interests of the USSR.

2 Stepped up arms aid to the various combatants or guerrilla elements operating within the states of the area, or between Marxist and non-Marxist states.

3 Rallying of the more "orthodox" members of the nonaligned group into a common anti-Israel, "anti-imperialist," and "progressive" camp — a "Two Worlds" policy mirroring the Zhdanov construction for Europe after World War II.

4 Encouraging of a new front and common working program between the Palestine-liberation forces, of various stripes, and the burgeoning Pan-Islamic movement given fresh inspiration by the revolution in Iran under the leadership of the Islamic Revolutionary council headed by Ayatollah Khomeini and the U.S.-Iranian tensions provoked by Teheran's taking of the U.S. hostages.

5 In Iran itself, arms aid to the separatist Kurd movement in the north bordering upon the USSR; covert assistance to elements loyal to the Tudeh (Communist) party and its "front" allies — ultimate aim of which is to convert the unstable "twin-rule" condition in Iran (which is analogous to the situation in Russia in 1917) into a species of militant Islamic-Marxist regime as a transition to a fully Marxist-Communist regime as exists, for example, in neighboring Afghanistan.

6 Pressure, largely by means of internal subversion via radical Islamists, upon Turkey, as a traditionally key "northern tier" country, in the age-old Russian urge to assert itself southwards and achieve unimpeded egress out of the Black Sea and past the Golden Horn into the crucial lake of the Mediterranean Sea.

In the light of the above, it is impossible to agree with those American spokesmen, many of whom are of left-wing persuasion, who insist that America need no longer be concerned over the global "Communist threat," which they place in quotation marks. For these people, the Cold War ended years ago; to them, any talk of a "world-historical" confrontation between the totalitarian world and its sympathizers and the democracies and their allies (natural or committed) is a red herring, archaic, even "anti-democratic" and "Cold-Warish." This kind of neo-isolationism, or is it defeatism and kitten-blindness? has been heard before in American history: It reflects either outright ignorance and naivete, or something worse — a sellout of their country in the name of misguided "progressivism," or whatever. At best, it is a luxury resulting from over a generation of welcome world peace, of the absence of full-scale world war, when America customarily wakes up (almost) too late. Perhaps we need to restore the myth of the Cold War — that is, recognize that we are engaged in a titanic struggle in which totalitarianism is on one side, liberal-democracy on the other.

Above all, the insular refusal to face up to the dangers confronting the free world and its friends blithely ignores the candid statements made by the enemies of freedom, especially those on the Marxist-Communist left. Malik's "World War III-has-already-begun" remark (see Chapter 15) epitomizes the motivation for the Soviets' positioning themselves geostrategically throughout the globe. As Brian Crozier has written, in *Strategy of Survival:* "The real Third World War has been fought and is being fought under our noses [but] few people have noticed what was going on."

It's time they did.

Chapter 18

Myth of "ETI"

"Our Sun is a strange, unique star that is surrounded by a
family of planets that are themselves a rarity in the realm of
stars . . . For the 'miracle' [of organic life] to occur, there
must be the rarest concurrence of the most favorable of
circumstances . . . The probability of the occurrence is in-
finitesimally small . . . Equally unlikely is the probability
of the evolution of intelligent life let alone technologically-
developed life on any other planet."

Dr. I. S. Shklovsky,
Soviet astrophysicist

"Either the entire Galaxy is teeming with intelligent life and
hence our Solar System must have been colonized hundreds
of millions of years ago, or there are no other inhabitants in
our Solar System, and, hence, most probably neither anywhere else in the Galaxy, placing man in a unique
position."

Dr. Michael D. Papagiannis,
American astronomer

Scientific hypotheses and theories are well-
organized myths. Thomas S. Kuhn, the well-known historian of
science and author of *The Structure of Scientific Revolutions*,
describes the way that major scientific turning-points in history

are only partly based upon observed "facts." Experiments, observations, measurements and other data — the factual parts of science — merely "articulate a paradigm," Kuhn writes. By paradigm is meant an "accepted example" of scientific practice and measurement, a "model" and "metaphysic" from which conflicting scientific schools of thought and traditions are formed. The world has known many such systems of scientific paradigms: Aristotelian, Ptolemaic, Newtonian, Cartesian, Einsteinian. Professor Kuhn, and other historians of science, like W. C. Dampier, J. W. N. Sullivan, Sir Arthur Eddington, and E. A. Burtt, note the way in which deductive reasoning and the scientific imagination are the most crucial factors in the making of scientific discoveries and revolutions. These authors explode the fallacy that the data, or "facts," dictate the various conclusions and inferences of science. The Dickensian Mr. Gradgrind's love of facts to the contrary, collection of data is a mere *duty* of the scientist; the virtue of the scientist is showing how these inputs of data are interpreted, or for that matter, just how they were selected and measured in the first place, and according to which theoretical frame. If facts merely dictated while scientists copied them down, wouldn't the scientists reach similar conclusions? All the numerous "schools" and conflicting theories in science would disappear and a single, monolithic Truth would emerge!

No such thing happens, of course. The same range of phenomena do *not* "produce" similar theories, conclusions, or stimulate identical hypotheses at the same or different times. On the contrary, natural science, no less than the social sciences and the humanities, stimulates a whole plethora of schools, interpretations, methods of measurement, hypotheses, etc., about the world. As Nelson Goodman puts it, all scientists and philosophers worth their salt are actually engaged in "world-making." That is, they create worlds out of their fertile minds and imaginations, the schemas, basic theoretical formulations, even metaphors by which lesser scientists organize their data and draw their conclusions — making the facts fit their presuppositions, in the process. All this "works" until the next scientific genius comes along.

For example, Isaac Newton imagined a world of solid bodies moving in orbits and attracting each other according to various laws. In the space between the bodies, Newton imagined a void filled with "the ether." Light, he thought, traveled through this jelly-like medium in the form of tiny corpuscles. Moreover, to Newton there was a Universal Time, an apparently cosmic Big Ben wound up and set by God.

Now, these theories worked for over 200 years — with the exception of a few critical assessments and counter-theories that occasionally arose. But by the time Einstein carefully untied the beautiful bows knotted by Dr. Newton, little was left of Newtonianism as a unifying theory of science, as a cosmology. One sacred Newtonian cow after the other was done away with by Einstein, who said: Time is relative to the observer, there being no G.S.T., or God Standard Time; light is not corpuscular, nor is there any medium like ether; electromagnetic, not gravitational, forces are among the crucial determiners of the paths followed by heavenly bodies in space.

Without a doubt, some day Einstein's paradigm of a space-time continuum will be undone by an imaginative genius. On the basis of the 2,000-year history of science and scientific guesstimates, we may be sure that paradigms for organizing observations of our world and of the universe will be produced by man in never-ending succession. And they will continue to clash with the systems that preceded them, just as Einstein's theories did with those of Newton.

What is true of the paradigms and metaphors of physics and astrophysics is doubly true of the systems developed in the more speculative sciences and humanities — philosophy, economics, psychology, history, cosmology. Yet, some of the practitioners within these disciplines display the incredible, metaphysical arrogance to proclaim that their pet theories are "undeniable," that this or that inference is "inevitable." Cheap money drives out sound currency: Today the pressures of pop-culture simplicity encourage the cheapening of the scientific coin. It is no exaggeration to say that pop-sci has threatened to replace serious and cautious scientific investigation in many crucial areas. Too often, the more reckless dogmatic representatives of the "scientific community" — which in many respects is neither scientific nor a community — obtain the interviews in the weekly newsmagazines and the science pages of newspapers and thus impose their views upon the public. Or *The New York Times* squanders a sizable sum of money, as it did a few years ago, on a futile attempt to prove the existence of the "Loch Ness Monster" in Scotland. "Nessie," of course, didn't appear, but this did not stop *The Times* from investing still more money in a continuation of this fruitless "zoological" search. Equally undaunted, the partisans of USOs, Big Foot, mysteries of the Bermuda Triangle, and their millions of duped followers continue dogmatically to proclaim their "findings" as scientific truth.

Shall we dismiss all this as harmless "shlock" that sells books or newspapers and titillates naive readers? I refuse to downgrade the importance of pseudo-science, because I detect the devastating effect it is having on the minds of so many people, especially the young.

Some years ago, a group of concerned writers, philosophers, and scientists also became alarmed, so they formed a society of likeminded persons whose purpose was to expose pop-sci literature as bogus science (despite the embarrassment this might cause certainly duly-registered scientists and professors). Thus, the Committee for the Scientific Investigation of Claims of the Paranormal, and its publication, *The Zetetic,* now work overtime to demythologize UFOlogy, astrology, clairvoyance, Kirlian photography, ESP, the Bermuda Triangle myths, psychokinesis, and dozens of other harmless or harmful myths. The committee has received enthusiastic support from a cluster of trustworthy philosophers, scientists, and writers — among them Sidney Hook, W. V. Quine, Philip J. Klass, George Abell. Unfortunately, the list of "Fellows" of the committee happens to include the likes of Isaac Asimov, and Carl Sagan, of Cornell. Both of these popular writers surely must be classed among the populizers of highly questionable, I would say harmful, myths — in their case, about the Universe. In confidential correspondence with me, one of the better-known members of this committee deplored the membership in the group of some individuals who did not actually subscribe to the purposes of the committee, and he included Sagan in this category.

Of all the myths propagated by the pop-sci crowd, ETI (Extra-terrestrial Intelligence) is to me the most harmful because its "field" is so vast, involving as it does astrophysics and religion, man's perception of the cosmos and of himself in the most profound sense.

First, the self-assuredness of the ETI crowd is overwhelming. Writing in *Science Digest* in June 1974, Asimov went so far as to say that the emergence of life on our biosphere was the "inevitable result of high-probability chemical reactions." (I'll get to the "probability" myth in a moment, but note here "inevitable.") In *TV Guide,* which assured the professor of an extremely wide as well as gullible audience, Sagan pontificated: There is an "abundance of technical civilizations in the Galaxy" and they are "probably a few hundred light years away," picking up worn-out TV programs like Milton Berle and Howdy Doody, which were aired a generation ago of Earth's time. Joining these publications — with similar inevitability and dogmatism about ETI — were or are *The Reader's Digest* (a later piece, however, took everything back), *National Geographic, Scientific American,* and science columns in newspapers too numerous to mention (but including such science writers as Walter Sullivan and Robert C. Cowen, of *The Times* and *The Christian Science Monitor,* respectively). In a *Times* Sunday magazine article in 1978, Sagan claimed — and with this I must agree — that belief in ETI was now the "majority view," overwhelmingly so, worldwide. Far from deploring this, Sagan relished it. I don't.

Second, think of what ETI claims and of the unproven basis for its claims; think also about the results of the claims, for human consciousness. According to ETI, humanoid intelligence is like a cosmic weed growing all over the Universe. Humankind is xeroxable, the "inevitable" result of chemical reactions that are really quite predictable. As Sagan has put it, with all those billions of Sun-like stars "out there," isn't it reasonable to assume — "on the basis of probability" — that circling around these "Suns" are planets, among whom "must be" Earth-like worlds? Nothing special about Earth or man, or intelligent animals quite like him, copiously populating the Universe in extraterrestrial "civilizations" that may well exceed ours in every respect (it is to be hoped, not in arrogance).

Finally, the only "inevitable" thing about the ETI theory is that it inevitably degrades man's special status. It also gives the impression that Earth's evolution is a simple, common affair, whereas a number of scientists on the authentic, ultraviolet band of repute — as opposed to the infra-red status of the pop-scientists — describe our biosphere's evolution as unique and "irreversible." They view our evolution, especially that mysterious jump from inorganic to organic life form, as akin to an extremely complicated baseball game in which it would be impossible to repeat or duplicate all the plays, accidents, and chance happenings inning-by-inning that led to the final score. The whole "game" is *sui generis* and unrepeatable. Similarly, at each stage in the 4.5 billion years of Earth's history, certain events, many of them contingent on other chance happenings, conspired to produce certain results, most of which themselves are not clearly understood. What is understood, in part, is that Earth's discrete distance from the Sun, the peculiar magnetic field that it possesses, the periodic venting of its gaseous and molten core, the probability that Earth suffered some "helpful," unique accidents within the Solar System, its size and mass, and countless other characteristics all provided a potential Garden of Eden in which

Earth's possibly unparalleled, unique drama was played. The point is that this anti-ETI scenario is possible — if one can believe a host of scientists who just now are beginning to come forward and challenge the ETI group, whose reign has outlasted its use. (Among new ETI critics is astronomer Michael H. Hart, who in 1979 did a computer analysis of "hypothetical planets," resembling Earth, and found that far from being a common affair, Earth-like civilized life is "exceedingly rare" and the one we have on Earth "may even be unique.")

Another astronomer, and former devotee of ETI, I. S. Shklovsky, of the Soviet Union, recently performed the rare feat of reversing his position by 180°, despite the fact that official Soviet Diamat (dialectical materialism) demands the cold, materialistic, cosmic-weed theory of cosmogeny and cosmology. Since his article in *Voprosy Filosofii* late in 1978 (see quote beginning this chapter), Dr. Shklovsky, once co-author with Sagan of a 1966 book promoting ETI, has argued the case for Earth's possible uniqueness. (Oddly, Sagan has made no comment about Comrade Shklovsky's turnabout, possibly because the free-enterprise system in the United States extends to marketable science as well as to goods and services: Sagan's ETI obviously sells a lot of books and articles in these outer-space happy times.)

I am not the only person who perceives a distinctly misanthropic, political, and ideological stance in the pro-ETI position. In one of the major books of this century, *Chance & Necessity,* written by the Nobel Prize-winning biochemist, Jacques Monod, the insightful Frenchman describes Diamat and its baneful influence on certain aspects of modern science as an updated form of harmful "animism," obscurantism, and nonscience. Marxist-Leninist materialism "projects into inanimate nature," Monod writes, regularity, "laws," purpose, etc., which in fact are not in nature. Diamat even imagines regularity, laws, purpose, and a law-bound "process" in man's social, economic and political life! Thus, by Diamat logic, "Socialism" becomes the inevitable product of the "historical process." Likewise, ETI becomes the "law-bound" result of the processes of chemistry, physics, and biology, and is "inevitable."

To this Monod responds, sadly, that ideology has taken the place of science; determinists, of the Diamat school, merely project human consciousness, reason, and purpose onto the dumb physical world, which itself is "governed" merely by chance and contingency. Materialistic-minded animists endow the physical world with the humanoid qualities of reason, purpose, will. This myth, he says, leads to all sorts of egregious errors — among them the notion that Earth's experience is common. The Universe, says, Monod, is "not pregnant with life." Our biosphere does "not contain a predictable class of objects or of events but constitutes a particular occurrence [and] unpredictable." Man, he warns, must realize, sooner or later, that he likely dwells in "total solitude," that his residence in the Universe may well be one of "fundamental isolation." *We May Be Alone* is perhaps a more apt title for *Time*'s writer Walter Sullivan's book.

Viewed against Dr. Monod's strictly *non*-religious argument for Earth's and Earth life's likely uniqueness, the argument of the dialectical materialists, and of Sagan & Co., look like the emotional whimpers of children who dread the prospect of solitude. After all, the Universe may *not* turn out to be a gigantic kibbutz, Gemeinschaft, Moscow, or Cornell, populated with intelligent or even unintelligent creatures, the latter of which are probably under a monopoly by our own planet. *Earth may be a uniquely-situated place for the infinitesimally-chancey arrivals of tenuous humanoid, mammalian, or even plant life.* Monod, for one, is not afraid to imagine that Earth was merely lucky — or unlucky, if we don't watch our ways — in the series of accidents that took place here, under the rarest of circumstances. Monod's is a brave stand, but one that contrasts with the religionists' argument for Earth's uniqueness based upon the notion that God performed a miracle and that our biosphere was a pre-planned paradise for the creation of man.

Just how plausible is this allegedly "predictable," "inevitable" evolution that took place on Earth? Biochemistry, Monod's field, is, among other things, the study of the relationship between organic and inorganic life and their processes. Biochemistry is distinctly interested in studying the transition between inert, inorganic non-life to reproductive, living organic life — a riddle of our evolution that has never been solved. From their bio-chemical perspective why do Monrod and others find Earth's experience to have been so rare and complex?

All living things, without exception, are composed of two main classes of macromolecular components: proteins and nucleic acids. The same is true of "residues," a finite number of which are also found in all living beings on Earth: 20 amino acids for the proteins, 4 nucleotides for the nucleic acids. Moreover, all the organisms — up to and including man — perform largely the same sequence of reactions and chemical operations, as Monod explains, "the mobilization and storage of chemical potential, the biosynthesis of cellular components," of which human metabolism is an example. The invariance of, or similarity within, the various species on Earth is guaranteed by the DNA nucleotide sequences, a kind of "code," or "text," by which hereditary traits are established through the genes and chromosomes. Genetic coding is performed through the complex double-helixes of DNA molecules — "stereo-chemical language," Monod explains — each of whose "letters" consists of a sequence of three nucleotides (a triplet) in the DNA, specifying one amino acid (among 20) in the polypeptides.

The above coding guarantees the distinctiveness of a species. What, then, permits changes to occur, so that a new species may arrive on the scene and perhaps be better adapted to the changing environmental circumstances? Actually, the genetic system is so set up as to permit, as it were, "errors" to occur. These "accidents" amount to a "scrambling" of the genetic code, through inversion, displacement, and external shocks upon the formation of the molecular chains. "Chance alone," Monod declares, "is at the source of every innovation [and] at the very root of the stupendous edifice of evolution." Mutations are examples of these chance happenings.

As to the chemical makeup of the amino acids and nucleotides, they are fairly easy to obtain — compounds identical or analogous to these have been fabricated in laboratories. "Primordial soups" have been made into which a high-voltage "lightning bolt" has been introduced (not unlike Mary Shelley's imagined feat in Dr. Frankenstein's mountaintop laboratory) in order to obtain organic "building blocks." But a missing ingredient in such soups deprives them of the importance that has too often been given them in ETI and other literature: namely, the formation of macromolecules which are capable of *promoting their own replication*. Nor, of course, has "protoplasm" — living substance — ever been made in laboratories. As Monod states, bluntly: "We have no idea what the structure of a primitive cell might have been." These so-called "primitive" cells — like the billion-year-old viruses — employ genetic codes and other complex mechanisms, or the "chemical ground plan," that resembles the infinitely-complicated mechanism existing in human cells. "Primitive" is thus an unsuitable word to describe these early precursors of organic evolution.

Adding to the complexity of cellular genetics is the role played by enzymes. These are catalyst-molecules that facilitate the chemical reactions that are necessary for the various metabolisms, defenses of a cell's life, etc., to occur. Laboratory experiments — such as Urey's lightning bolts at the University of

Chicago in the 1950's or Oparin's soups in the USSR somewhat later — have never produced anything more than compounds that vaguely resembled the so-called building-blocks of life on earth, and never any enzymes. Nor have they been able to duplicate Earth's primordial environment under which life originated (even the pure chemicals used today are vastly different from the impure ones that prevailed on Earth billions of years ago). The scientific relevancy of such experiments is stoutly questioned, for example, in the book by the British scientist, Robert E. D. Clark, *The Universe: Plan or Accident?* Yet, these "soups" occupy an important niche in the cookbooks of ETI chefs.

The simplistic notion that life may be "easily" created in a laboratory or throughout the Universe is also accompanied by simplistic mathematics and statistics. When Sagan says, oracularly, that billions of "Sun-like stars" in the universe "must have" Earth-like planets encircling them, he is indulging in what Mark Twain called "lies, damned lies" — that is, statistics.

In computing probabilities — such as that seven will be rolled by a pair of dice — the *countable parameters of probability must be known*. That is, when you toss a well-balanced penny and expect that heads will come up half the time (if you toss it many, many times), you base your 50/50 odds on the *fact* that the penny has only two faces, heads and tails. Likewise, with a deck of 52 cards, the probability of drawing an ace or a face-card or some other ticket can be computed on the basis of the *known number* of such cards within the 52-card pile, if enough drawings are performed. Fine. But what if the "parameters," or odds, are limitless, or, at least, so large that they cannot be counted or predicted? What are the chances, say, of finding an identical grain of sand on the beach at Coney Island? One in a trillion, a trillion trillion? Is it possible that you would *never* find a similar, let alone identical, grain of sand at Coney? Doubtlessly, not, or at least it gives you a headache to imagine it. The fact it that when the "gamble" involves huge odds, *it clearly is impossible even to formulate such odds with any definiteness*.

The estimation of the chances of there being life elsewhere in the Universe is like the grains of sand on the beach: The factors working against the existence of extraterrestrial life vastly outnumber the factors working *for* this kind of life, and the factors working for it are at once rare and particular, accidental, and dependent on an irreversible sequence of timed events dating back to Earth's earlier existence (about which little is known in any case). Professor Sagan thus plays the role of God, or one of his better-informed cherubim, when he claims to be able to estimate the odds for reproducing Earth's experience Universewide. He ignores the overwhelming odds against producing life, or its capability of eking out a life if one were produced, in this forbidding, inhospitable Universe. "Making it," the way Earth did, is about like an automobile traveling a world-girdling highway with billions of intersections crossing it, while running red traffic lights along the way, but without colliding with a single crossing automobile! As an erstwhile materialist believer in a rather predictable origination of life, J. D. Bernal, once phrased it: "It would have been much easier to discuss how life didn't originate than how it did."

The crowning embarrassment inflicted on all ETI believers are the photographs taken by interplanetary, and cislunar, orbiting craft sent on research missions in space in recent years. The Moon, Mars, Venus, Mercury, Jupiter, and Saturn have all been mapped with amazing clarity; chemical sampling of soil has also been carried out on some of the missions. Result: barren worlds staring dumbly at us like skulls with craters for eye-sockets. What were supposed — even by Galileo — to be "seas" or "canals," on Mars or on the Moon, have turned out to be leprous scores and fissures left behind after volcanic eruptions or flood-plaining of their surfaces by a kind of "lava." Lately, Sagan has begun to admit that our Solar System may contain no life other than on Earth. Yet, it was Sagan who made just the opposite claim a few years back and who, if he were making observations of our Solar System from one of those distant planets he imagines to revolve about a remote "Sun," would claim that our Solar System "teemed" with life.

I am certainly not opposed to keeping the radio-telescope discs turned on, pointed at Alpha Centauri or wherever it is suspected that a "Sun-like star" may be flourishing like Old Sol in the fathomless depths of the Universe, with "planets" obscuring its face. But I really do not expect to hear a broadcast of that "second most important news story," after the Second Coming — namely, that an extraterrestrial civilization is communicating with us from outer space. Granted, *confirmed* existence of ETI could well have a healthy influence on us provincial earthlings — with our national-liberation struggles, "punishing" border wars, terrorism and bloodletting that masquerade as heroic humanitarianism, boat people, hostage-taking, orthodox ideologies whose heretics are committed to insane asylums or labor camps, and totalitarianisms that are so dishonest as to claim that they are true democracies.

Meanwhile, it seems to me harmful to assume that

we are "definitely" not alone, that we, or other "humanoids," grow weed-like throughout the Milky Way Galaxy and the Universe as a whole. Such a belief blithely ignores the strong possibility of Earth's uniqueness and demeans the human coin by depicting mankind as a rather predictable collision of atoms and molecules — The atomist-materialist Lucretius *redux!*

As for me, I prefer the double-helix of skepticism about ETI. Which I combine with the unseen hope that man will cherish and conserve his Earthly home as he guards the tenuous skein of civilization that he has managed somehow to weave here, despite implacable enemies. If this be myth, it is, at least, a helpful one.

CONCLUSION . . .

Chapter 19

Faith and Will

> ". . . I will go a step further with my will, not only act with it,
> but believe as well; believe in my individual reality and
> creative power."
>
> William James

At a time when myths that might give our culture vitality have been debunked, when our heroes are toppled like Humpty Dumpty, when legends are dismissed as shams, how, it might be asked, can we resurrect or create beneficial myths that invigorate the nation? Clearly, the chapters that have been presented are essentially descriptive and only indirectly prescriptive. But the answer to the question is implicit in the problem. We possess the capacity to be powerless or potent; to admire our accomplishments or dismiss them. Ultimately, we determine our future through our faith in ourselves and our will to act.

Faith and will, because they are inspirational terms, possess the capacity for extreme responses, responses which can be tyrannical. One can be engulfed by the will to dominance in the absence of moral precepts and one can be totalitarian when faith is unrestrained by tolerance and decency.

What is required — it seems to us — is a free will that inherently imposes moral order. Instead of the will to dominance, the very privilege of willing demands an Augustinian morality which inhibits dehumanizing action. Yet, it is traditional morality which in the modern age has been seen as the enemy of free will. Our literature canonizes liberation over moral precepts. Psychoanalysis — wittingly or unwittingly — undermined traditional moral behavior. Instead of emphasizing honor and virtue, psychoanalysis introduced the "science" of the unconscious, a science which vitiated will. To speak of morality invites the charge of uptightness, a pejorative that is not easily renounced without the renunciation of morality itself. Yet, notwithstanding this argument, moral will exists at the center of our lives. We do discriminate between good and bad behavior — even though the standards are often unclear and the culture relegates all acts to relativistic rationalizations.

The myth of free will can support and, indeed, validate a social and moral order if the will does not arbitrarily legislate what is good and bad. What appears to us in this claim is the irony of freedom: We are free only when constrained by moral standards. We are free only when our essence — our true selves — can be shown as it is. Freedom is a condition created by its restraints; it is not opposed by morality but complemented by it. Empirical evidence supports the conclusion that a constraining moral order is a necessary prerequisite for free will. Puritanism established the ground work for constitutional liberty as the morality of Greek gods invited Periclean democracy. In the Judeo-Christian tradition one comes to God by relinquishing will. But in the act of "letting go" one rediscovers free will. Through a willful act of selecting God man is bound to morality yet truly free. It would be a fatuous exercise to believe in moral will without also having faith in God. For if there is no God, morality is whatever you want it to be, including its own elimination.

Faith has its own rewards. It can uplift the spirit or depress it. But it is inextricably connected with will. William James wrote: "My first act of free will shall be to believe in free will." His faith preceded and gave his will inspiration. What emerges from James' studies and what has a direct bearing on mythic structure is the emergence of action from faith. A faith in freedom results in acts that affirm freedom's existence. A faith in the future leads to behavior that confirms the existence of a future.

The enigma that confounds social analysts is what encourages faith in the first place? At a time when nihilism afflicts western life as an epidemic, there are no effective answers to this question. Utilitarian responses don't suffice. Once again we must return to religion. For from religion springs the eternal questions about life's meaning. But religion is not learned like some equation. It does not become plausible through cognition. It relies on ritual, on prayer, on self discovery. One cannot know what is believed; one simply believes. Conviction is established by repeating the ritual. Pascal urged that man multiply his contacts with the unknown so that he might benefit from the privileges of God's bounty. To quote again Isaac Bashevis Singer's contention: "Whenever I am in trouble, I pray. And since I'm always in trouble, I pray alot. Even when you see me eat and drink, while I do this, I pray." As a character in one of Singer's short stories notes: "Belief in itself is beneficial. It is written that a good man lives by his faith." Repetition and practice constitute our experience more than we realize. It is the perseverance that motivates belief, a driving determination to do what was done before.

But what comes first, the will or the faith? Can will exist without faith? Can faith exist without will? They obviously cannot be separated like chaff and husk. In the ritual of prayer they merge. The power of prayer is that it renews inner strength. All of the challenges to our faith made by science and technology cannot undermine that. For prayer — in the several forms it assumes — contains a structure that awakens our consciousness to the inner meaning of life and reality itself.

Action, as opposed to activity, is an historical conception saturated with a point of view, a direction. It is — as we've suggested — a proof of being, since it is part of an epoch of becoming, becoming in the sense of personal development and historical evolution. As Arnold Toynbee illustrated, civilizations rise and fall on their ability to believe in themselves. Can we accept Macbeth's words?

"Life's but a waking shadow, a poor player
   That struts and frets his hour upon the stage
   And then is heard no more: it is a tale
   Told by an idiot, full of sound and fury,
   Signifying nothing."

We think not. All of us require a faith in ourselves in order to survive. If life is a mere burlesque, then there is no meaning, no need for faith. This, we submit, man cannot tolerate. Men and women delineate meaning as they engage life. Even the futile and sterile acts teach us lessons. In *The Myth of Sisyphus* Albert Camus writes, "Each atom of that stone, each mineral flake of that night-filled mountain, in itself forms a world. The struggle itself toward the heights is enough to fill a man's heart. One must imagine Sisyphus happy.''

At the moment Americans are not impressively happy. Nor is there any indication that we have enough faith in ourselves or the will to act forthrightly in our own interests. We suggest to the rest of the world a country not eager to engage events but, instead, prone to withdraw from difficult decisions. The lack of faith manifests itself as lethargy. We have lost our direction because we have lost our ability to believe. We act aimlessly because a myth — ritual faith in the future has not been practiced. Our morality suffers in direct proportion to an emphasis on liberationist solutions. We want a freedom without the constraints of God, ethics, and honor. We assume that greater production of goods will solve all our problems when it primarily masks our problems. We interpret success and happiness as tangible things which cannot give us what we really need. We flounder because our assumptions are naive, our national purpose forgotten.

These observations are not necessarily the view of cynics. It is because of an abiding faith in this nation that we despair over present conditions, while yet believing that the future can be bright. One unique and redeeming feature of the United States is that we Americans resist the iron grip of philosophical determinism. America's future, we insist, can be what we want it to be. However, this view imposes a responsibility to act, to act with the belief that our will can make a difference on the course of future events. The will to act, in fact, must be joined with a faith in ourselves. Without these conditions we will drift into the future and lament our powerlessness. We will seem like outcasts in a homeless world.

The answer to our future rests in our past. We had the power to choose what we became and we still have the power to choose what we become. In this contemporary age, we've been misguided into thinking there is either a "good life" *or* "a free life." B. F. Skinner's *Walden Two* may have something to do with the choice. But this isn't a choice from our tradition. We have believed that the good life was the free life, that unless individual will were permitted, the good life could not be attained. As we've noted, no person is completely free, but the myth of freedom is important to retain. Without it we are relegated to a primordial state in which we are conditioned to disregard the need for personal choice.

All of us are "conditioned" to some extent by the environment in which we find ourselves. But at some point we *choose* to be conditioned. For instance, a man acts to save a friend by risking his own life, not out of a conditioned response but through will. We must regain our will from the inventions and myth-fabrications that have weakened it; above all, from a naive belief that technology can solve all our problems. Consciousness surrendered cannot be regained. But a consciousness to change the world around us can be the handmaiden for social action. Perhaps what we first require is evidence that a struggle is going on. For if we sweat and strain to engage life's problems, we can be so inspired by our own efforts that desired results might follow. But even if they don't follow, the knowledge that Americans realized and accepted the challenge, that they struggled for their beliefs, is what Camus meant when he suggested that Sisyphus was happy. Nothing worthwhile comes without paying a price. Sacrifice, suffering, and death are the classic requisites for redemption. Comfort, ease, and the immortal life are merely the ingredients for a Devil's brew of meaningless existence.

What we propose is a national effort to rediscover our myths, particularly those myths that gave grandeur to this nation. In answering the question Crevecoeur asked almost two centuries ago, "What is an American?" scholars and laymen relied on a mythology of industry, achievement, faith in the future, and man's unexplored potentialities. For America was a land becoming, a New World unencumbered by orthodoxies. Anything could be explored here — a new social arrangement or a new technology. This was, indeed, an Eden for adventurers.

Our present state is due in no small part to the loss of this vision. We criticize ourselves unmercifully; we bear guilt for matters we cannot control; we have emasculated our national will with demeaning exhortations of our alleged mistakes. The present national course is suicidal. But it is no accident. Every myth that sustained our spirit has been shattered. For example, rational educators tell us that it is silly to believe that George Washington cut down the cherry tree or that Paul Bunyon felled timber with one swing of his axe. Or, social scientists continually try to convince us this is not a land of opportunity. Journalists, searching for the dark underbelly of our national life, write exclusively about executive philandering, white-collar crimes and government shenanigans. Television news programming is devoted to murder, rape, fire, destruction, and natural disasters. If one relied on television exclusively for information, it would be easy to believe apocalypse is around the corner. The result is that our collective imagination is reduced by narrowly conceived rational explanations for all phenomena. And our hopes are interred by grave-diggers who remind us that historical forces have passed us by.

That we believe this nonsense is our nightmare. We have been made powerless by our national false myths. Although we are the most powerful nation on earth, we don't have the will to protect our interests. In fact, we no longer seem able to define our interests. We have resilient institutions and vibrant industries, yet presentations on our media are preoccupied with the relentless Red Bear who lives in a society where nothing works but the military. We are afraid, but for the wrong reasons. We seem incapable of acting because no one or no cause can inspire us. We shrink in size as our self-perception is reduced.

The key to this national dilemma is remembrance. Our history was no accident. Great accomplishments resulted from great visions. As much as our view of ourselves has been seen through a prism of distorted values, the United States represents the only place where individual freedom can be retained, where problems affecting the globe may be solved, where enterprise and achievement are rewarded. When Simone DeBeauvoir wrote about America in the fifties her book was not an unequivocal endorsement of our way of life. She contended that while there was much she loathed, there was also something that fascinated her: "the tremendous opportunities . . . the gigantic risks." Her statement is still worth recalling as we enter a new decade in our history:

"All human problems are posed here on a tremendous scale; they will be solved here, but whether we will find these problems, in retrospect, greatly clarified or buried in the darkness of indifference depends largely on the solutions themselves. Yes, I think that is what moved me so strongly as I took my departure. America is one of the world's pivotal points: the future of man is at stake here. To like America, or not to like her: these words are meaningless. Here is a battlefield, and one can only be stirred by the struggle she carries on within herself, a struggle whose stakes are beyond measure."

To struggle, to engage problems, to look to the future armed with moral courage, to be at the center of events — this should be our lesson for the world. From it a myth was created. Like a prayer or ritual that we no longer enjoin, it has lost its vitality. Still, all is not lost. Our traditions, at least, remain as constant reminders of what we once had. As a nation, we need to remember those myths that gave us strength. Then, we might take them up once again.

GLOSSARY

Cited below are definitions of words employed throughout the book. In keeping with our polemical purpose the definitions are contentious and wry. They also reveal something — we believe — about the state of our present mythologies.

Alienation: rationalization for detached self-indulgence.

Anti anti-communist: liberals who are so open minded they can only oppose those opposed to Communists.

Balance of Power: the point of equilibrium at which American military descent meets Soviet ascent.

Behaviorism: Explaining human action on the basis of experiments with pigeons, grey-lag geese, or chimps.

Bourgeois: a term widely applied by Marxists or the naive to such sacred things as the American Revolution, democracy, or private property.

Competition: an idea that once inspired excellence; now believed to be a cause of neurosis; its elimination means we do have less excellence, but the same can't be said of neurosis.

Conservative: a term used as a pejorative by liberals because conservatives refuse to accept the changes liberals propose.

Contemporary Work Ethic: an urge to do productive work which, however, may be resisted either by lying down until the urge passes, or by accepting welfare.

Democracy: that form of government which allows 51% of the population to tell the other 49% how it should conduct it affairs.

Detente: for the Soviets, the making of war with proclamations of peace; for Americans, avoiding war with proclamations of peace.

Determinism: predicting the course of all human affairs through the crystal ball of ideology.

Economy of Scale: the belief that larger productive capacity can be more efficient than smaller counterparts: an idea that has been altered by the conception that smaller is better, even when less efficient and more costly.

Equality: substituting the arbitrariness of nature with the arbitrariness of man.

Fairness: when I get the advantage and you get what's left.

Free Speech: what some want for themselves but refuse to grant to others.

Freudianism: all the arguments that would have embarrassed Freud or prompted him to label them neurotic.

Geopolitics: a blend of geography and politics once given a bad name by the Nazi Dr. Karl Haushofer, who mistook the German "Heartland" for the genuine article, the Russian Heartland.

Good Life: what the free life used to be.

Government Regulation: the assumption that someone sitting in a Washington office knows what's good for you, even if you have to pay to find out what that might be.

Happiness: what the media describes in vivid details and which, when tried, simply leaves you with an unhappy and perpetual hangover.

Hippie: a latterday cynic, skeptic, or other Dionysian dropout who becomes avant-garde merely by being militantly eccentric; or, *Weekend Hippie,* hoi-polloi who ape the true Hippies by staying up all night one day of the week wearing long hair, and sporting love beads.

History: faith in the tangible existence of the dead past.

Humanitarianism: doing inhuman acts with the justification they are for humane ends.

Human Potential Movement: a movement that destroys the potential to do anything human, except engage in guilt-free sexual encounters.

Immorality: whatever you think is bad, ergo, whatever is incompatible with the national credo, you accept.

Inflation: what a lack of work, hedonism, government spending, and an increased money supply produce.

Kremlinology: the arcane non-science of predicting the predictable — namely, that the new rulers in Moscow will continue the misanthropic policies of their predecessors.

Laissez-faire: letting the morally-neutral response of the market-place determine the standards of the culture.

Liberal: a term used as a pejorative by conservatives, because conservatives won't accept changes liberals have proposed. (see *Conservative*).

Liberationist: using personal freedom as an absolute standard for the evaluation of all social questions.

Liberty: a precious value that has been devalued by those who squander it on extreme actions.

Manners: an antideluvian concept designed to promote social order; now seen as an attempt at fascist despotism.

Marxism: statements attributed to Marx, some of which he never made, others of which he wished he had not made.

The Military: people in olive-drab who follow orders given by people in mufti.

Moral Relativism: "On the one hand, but on the other . . ."; "that's your opinion, I have my opinion . . ."; "that might be wrong but you have to understand the social context of that event . . ."; etc.

Nationalization: taking by force, or quasi-legal means, what thieves take through sleight of hand.

Negotiations: the point after which all your concessions have been made and the Soviets agree to bargain.

Neoconservative: disenchanted former liberals.

Pluralism: many groups fighting for an equal slice of the proverbial national pie, accompanied by shrinkage of the pie.

Pot: a proven harmful drug, like alcohol, which distorts the mind and gives the partaker an excuse for his or her own lack of talent, imagination, or a sense of humor.

Potency: an 80-year-old whose sexual prowess is unaffected by saltpeter or attending sex-therapy sessions.

Recession: what inevitably occurs after inflation.

Religion: what psychology and/or encounter sessions have replaced as an expression of faith.

Revolution: as in revolving doors: an uneven exchange of one group of rulers for a worse one.

S.A.L.T.: talks to limit strategic arms as well as a substance the Soviets put in the open wound of an enemy or on tails of their adversaries.

Socialist: part of the title of the Nazi Party and of the Soviet dictatorship.

Success: everything you dreamed of having and cannot achieve.

Taxes: an attempt to convince the public that it has no right to the money it has worked hard to obtain.

Television: a plugged-in, turned on, play of light, dark and colored shadows and images signifying whatever you want it to.

Terrorism: "heroic" inhumanity to man.

Truth: conclusions about something in perpetual motion or change; the incredible miracle whereby Heraclitus steps in and out of the river while he and the river remain unchanged.

Two-party System: as natural to Americans as the "ins" and "outs" of two competing teams in baseball.

United Nations: a step in the wrong direction toward a World State which is even a bigger mistake.

Violence: the way children get their way by throwing blocks and adults theirs by throwing bricks or firing bullets.

Work Ethic: an anachronism based on an equally old-fashioned idea that there are rewards only for hard work and good deeds.

World State: a man-made Frankenstein monster as unnatural, unmanageable, or menacing as Mary Shelley's fictitious artifact.